"I love devotionals that are real, that pull us to the heart of our needs. In our crazy busy lives, we need devotionals to efficiently and effectively use scripture and writings that speak to our deepest emotions and longings. I especially love devotionals that direct us to the One who can meet our every need—and that One is our faithful Father. In *Day-Votions® with Your Faithful Father*, Rebecca Barlow Jordan has written a wonderful devotional that does just that. The layout includes responses from the Father's heart, directed to our needs; and then our responses back. With each devotion targeted to specific needs, Rebecca includes pertinent scriptures and challenges, as well as places to journal. Thank you, Rebecca, for writing this wonderful devotional that will enrich the spiritual lives of many."

Nancie Carmichael, author of *The Unexpected Power of Home* (and many other books)

"For fans of *Jesus Calling*, this little book will be an intimate new way for you to connect with the heart of God. In a chaotic world, we all need to know more than ever before what will never change. Rebecca Barlow Jordan beautifully reminds us of who God is and how he loves us are forever the same."

Holley Gerth, bestselling author of *What Your Heart Needs for the Hard Days*

"*Day-votions® with Your Faithful Father* is a stunning work that provides a biblical response to the struggles we all have as Christians. Rebecca Barlow Jordan thoughtfully put together 90 different scenarios, such as "When You Think You've Lost Your Way" and "When You Want to Give Up" and provides a *Jesus Calling* type of word from our Faithful Father. Her book, however, also gives the reader more: a scripted prayer for each reading ("From a Grateful Heart"), a daily truth, four different relevant Bible verses, and an opportunity for the reader to journal her thoughts and prayers. I love how this devotional book encourages the reader to dig into the scriptures and reflect about their power to overcome our negative thought life. I highly recommend this newest book in the Day-votions® series."

Janet Holm McHenry, author of 24 books including *The Complete Guide to the Prayers of Jesus*

"Packed with scripture, seasoned biblical teacher, Rebecca Barlow Jordan gives a glimpse of how to develop a deep, abiding, and strong bond with God, our Creator and Faithful Father in Heaven. *Day-votions® with Your Faithful Father, 90 Days with the One Who Wants to Meet All Your Needs*, will weave wisdom from the Word, with creative conversations and daily applications to personalize God's Word to your life in a meaningful, powerful, profoundly life-transforming way. Her *Daily Truth* segment and opportunity to respond to the multiple powerful verses each day will enrich your walk with the ONE who knows you and loves you most."

Pam Farrel, bestselling author of 54 books including co-authoring the award-winning *Discovering Hope in the Psalms: A Creative Bible Study Experience* and Co-Director of *Love-Wise*

"In *Day-votions® with Your Faithful Father*, Rebecca Barlow Jordan provides an intimate conversation between the reader and a loving parent. Beautifully crafted, it seems words from Heaven flowed through Rebecca's heart directly onto the pages. There is nothing lofty about this book. The daily content is relevant, kind, and thought-provoking, from the faithful Father's comments and the grateful reader's response to the daily truth and challenge. Each carefully selected daily reflection verse brings further life and love to the chapter. Overarching is the sense of deep joy and rich love evoked by these daily devotions."

Britt Yates Jones, Hardin-Simmons University Executive Director of Alumni Special Programs & Trustee Relations

DAY-VOTIONS® WITH YOUR FAITHFUL FATHER

Other Books by Rebecca Barlow Jordan

Marriage Toners
Courage for the Chicken Hearted
Eggstra Courage for the Chicken Hearted
At Home in My Heart
Daily in Your Presence
Daily in Your Presence Journal
Daily in Your Image
40 Days in God's Presence
40 Days in God's Blessing
Day-votions® for Women
Day-votions® for Mothers
Day-votions® for Grandmothers

DAY-VOTIONS® WITH YOUR FAITHFUL FATHER

90 Days with the One Who Wants to Meet All Your Needs

Rebecca Barlow Jordan

Copyright ©2022 by Rebecca Barlow Jordan

This title is also available as an eBook.

Published by Rebecca Barlow Jordan

Printed in the United States of America

All rights reserved. No part of this publication can be reproduced, stored in a retrieval system, or transmitted in any form or by any means—for electronic, mechanical, photocopy, recording, or any other—except for brief quotations in printed reviews, without the prior written permission of the author, Rebecca Barlow Jordan. You may contact her at **www.rebeccabarlowjordan.com** or **www.day-votions.com**.

All quotes and material set without a source are written by Rebecca Barlow Jordan. All rights reserved.

Day-votions® is a trademark of Rebecca Barlow Jordan.

ISBN 978-1-7377506-0-4

For a list of Bible versions and translations used, please see "Bible Versions and Translations," in the back of the book.

Cover and Interior Design by Raney Day Creative, LLC

To My Faithful Heavenly Father

Whom have I in heaven but you?
And earth has nothing I desire besides you.
My flesh and my heart may fail,
but God is the strength of my heart
and my portion forever.
Psalm 73:25-26 NIV

Contents

Introduction

Day 1	When You Need to Release the Past
	The One Who Gives You a Fresh Start
Day 2	When You Need Guidance
	The One Who Keeps You On Track
Day 3	When Disappoint Comes
	The One Who Never Disappoints
Day 4	When You Long to Make God Happy
	The One Who Takes Pleasure in You
Day 5	When You Need Encouragement
	The One Who Encourages the Discouraged
Day 6	When Your Heart Needs a Home
	The One Who Makes You Family
Day 7	When You Wonder If God Really Loves You
	The One Who Loves the Entire World
Day 8	When You Don't Know What to Do
	The One Who Teaches You What Is Good for You
Day 9	When You Need to Find Your Purpose
	The One Who Made You for His Glory
Day 10	When You're Tired of Trying
	The One Who Never Grows Tired or Weary
Day 11	When Fear Closes In
	The One Who Comforts You
Day 12	When Your God Isn't Big Enough
	The One Who Can Do Anything
Day 13	When You Want to Help Others Change
	The One Who Changes Lives

Day 14	When You Wonder About Your Worth	
	The One Who Calls You Priceless	
Day 15	When You Long for Deeper Intimacy with God	
	The One Who Satisfies You Completely	
Day 16	When God Seems Distant	
	The One Who Is Never Far from You	
Day 17	When Suffering Comes	
	The One Who Shares Your Suffering	
Day 18	When Loneliness Surrounds You	
	The One Who Will Never Leave You	
Day 19	When You Don't Understand God's Discipline	
	The One Who Disciplines Those He Loves	
Day 20	When You Feel Broken	
	The One Who Reshapes Your Life	
Day 21	When You Need to Hear from God	
	The One Who Hears and Answers Your Prayers	
Day 22	When You Need Stability	
	The One Who Never Changes His Mind	
Day 23	When You Need a Hero	
	The One Who Is Mighty to Save	
Day 24	When You Don't Know What to Pray	
	The One Who Intercedes for You	
Day 25	When You Need a Patient Father	
	The One Who Is Slow to Get Angry	
Day 26	When the Present Seems Like an Eternity	
	The One Who Inhabits Eternity	
Day 27	When the Future Seems Uncertain	
	The One Who Holds Tomorrow	
Day 28	When You Need a Friend	
	The One Who Makes You His Friend	
Day 29	When God's Creation Amazes You	
	The One Who Stretches Out the Heavens	
Day 30	When You Want to Flip Your Failures	
	The One Who Calls You Forward	

Day 31	When All You See Is Darkness
	The One Who Lights Your Darkness
Day 32	When Your Life Feels Empty
	The One Who Is Your Salvation and Joy
Day 33	When Life Doesn't Seem Fair
	The One Who Is Perfect and Just
Day 34	When Your Heart Needs Peace
	The One Who Gives True Peace
Day 35	When You Can't Find God
	The One Who Can Always Be Found
Day 36	When Your Vision Is Limited
	The One Who Opens Blind Eyes
Day 37	When It Seems God Is Sleeping
	The One Who Never Sleeps
Day 38	When You Crave God's Blessings
	The One Who Gives You Every Spiritual Blessing
Day 39	When You Desperately Need God's Help
	The One Who Is Ready to Help You
Day 40	When You've Wandered Away
	The One Who Will Heal Your Wayward Heart
Day 41	When You Need Order in Your Life
	The One Who Rules Over Everything
Day 42	When You Need Assurance You Are God's Child
	The One Who Whispers Reassurance to You
Day 43	When You Want Freedom from Sin's Control
	The One Who Offers Freedom
Day 44	When Your Work Seems Small
	The One Who Makes the Seed Grow
Day 45	When You Call Yourself a Nobody
	The One Who Uses Nobodies
Day 46	When You Need a Promise Keeper
	The One Who Always Keeps His Promises
Day 47	When You Need Courage
	The One Who Makes You Strong

Day 48	When You Struggle with Motives
	The One Who Examines All Motives
Day 49	When You Feel God Doesn't Need You
	The One Who Has No Needs
Day 50	When You Need to Forgive Yourself
	The One Who Forgives Completely
Day 51	When You Need a Shepherd
	The One Who Is Your Good Shepherd
Day 52	When You Need Someone to Catch Your Tears
	The One Who Wipes Away All Tears
Day 53	When Your Heart Cries for Justice
	The One Who Gives True Justice
Day 54	When You Want a Full Life
	The One Who Gives You Life
Day 55	When a Storm Is Brewing
	The One Who Calms Your Storms
Day 56	When You're Longing for Home
	The One Who Is Preparing a Place for You
Day 57	When You Want to Give Up
	The One Who Will Never Give Up On You
Day 58	When Grief Overwhelms You
	The One Who Is Acquainted with Grief
Day 59	When You're Walking Through the Fire
	The One Who Is Able to Deliver You
Day 60	When You Long for God's Grace and Goodness
	The One Whose Kindness Leads Us to Repentance
Day 61	When You Long for Godly Leaders
	The One Who Is Lord of Kings
Day 62	When You Need Divine Intervention
	The One Who Intervenes for You
Day 63	When Things Are Hard to Understand
	The One Whose Thoughts Are Not Your Thoughts
Day 64	When You Need God's Protective Covering
	The One Who Covers You with His Shadow

Day 65	When You Long to See God's Miracles
	The One Who Demonstrates His Holy Power
Day 66	When You Need to Remember Sin's Magnitude
	The One Who Took Your Punishment
Day 67	When You're Feeling Forgotten
	The One Who Will Never Forget You
Day 68	When You're Searching for Truth
	The One Who Exposes Lies
Day 69	When You're Feeling Anxious and Distressed
	The One Who Is Your Only Rock
Day 70	When You Don't Understand God's Mercy
	The One Who Is Rich in Mercy
Day 71	When Life Is a Confusing Mystery
	The One Who Reveals Mysteries
Day 72	When You Fear Not Having Enough
	The One Who Became Poor to Make You Rich
Day 73	When You Need a Warrior
	The One Who Is the Mighty Warrior
Day 74	When You're Stuck in the Now
	The One Who Is Eternal
Day 75	When You Think You've Lost Your Way
	The One Who Is the Only Way
Day 76	When You're Tempted to Be Judge and Jury
	The One Who Will One Day Judge the World
Day 77	When You Need to Renew Your Mind
	The One Who Transforms You
Day 78	When You Wonder About Your Destiny
	The One Who Gives You His Holy Spirit
Day 79	When You Need God's Healing Hand
	The One Who Heals You
Day 80	When You Need Someone to Talk To
	The One Who Invites You to Himself
Day 81	When You Need to Know God Cares
	The One Who Is Generous to All Who Ask

Day 82	When Your Gratitude Is Lacking
	The One Who Deserves Your Thanks
Day 83	When You Long to Know God As Your Father
	The One Who Adopts You As His Child
Day 84	When You Can't Feel God's Presence
	The One Who Is Everywhere
Day 85	When You Need Unfailing Love
	The One Whose Unfailing Love Never Ends
Day 86	When You're Feeling Needy
	The One Who Satisfies Every Need
Day 87	When You Want to Be More Than a Number
	The One Who Knows Your Name
Day 88	When Heaven Seems Near
	The One Who Will Take You to Heaven
Day 89	When You Long to Give God Praise
	The One Whose Name Is Above All Others
Day 90	When You're Longing for More Joy
	The One Who Makes Your Joy Overflow

Begin the Journey
Bible Versions and Translations
Acknowledgments
Notes
About the Author

Introduction

My desire to know God/Jesus began as a child when I would faithfully memorize Bible verses and read His Word daily. I decided to become a follower of Jesus at the age of eight. As a young mother, my thirst grew to an overwhelming passion to know and experience God on a deeper level. I read; I prayed; I listened, and I journaled.

From those disciplines grew another longing: to know and understand God's names, His character, His attributes, and His activity. The popular *Daily in Your Presence* series, as well as many of my books, grew out of that desire.

As I look back over my life, I can honestly say my Faithful Father has led me all the way. Both in failure and victory, I've experienced times when only He could have intervened—and did. Like you, I've known heartache and blessing, joy and pain. But as a day-voted follower of Jesus for decades, I can truly sum up my life's message in three words: *God is faithful*.

A. W. Tozer says, "God is faithful! He will remain faithful because He cannot change. He is perfectly faithful, because God is never partly anything. God is perfectly all that He is and never partly what He is. You can be sure that God will always be faithful. This faithful God, who never broke a promise and never violated a covenant, who never said one thing and meant another, who never overlooked anything or forgot anything, is the Father of our Lord Jesus and the God of the gospel. This is the God we adore…."[1]

God doesn't need to prove His faithfulness to us. All of creation can testify to His faithful character. As Tozer implied, God is faithful to the core. But I'm so grateful that God invites us to know His faithfulness in a thousand ways. Experiencing it through the meeting of our needs is only one of those ways.

I hope there will come a time when you will hunger for the presence of God as never before, and you will cry out passionately for His precious, healing touch. Long for it. Ask for it. Embrace the Heart Mender, the Thirst Quencher, the Joy Filler, and the Grace Giver. Come needy, and experience God's faithfulness today. You will never know how faithful God is until you experience Him for yourself.

A Personal Note to the Reader

Has God been faithful to you? Does He care about you and your needs? How do you know? Can you really talk to Him like a Father? What does it mean to be His child? Is it possible to sit down and commune with God as an intimate friend? And what do you say to Him? Why would a holy God even want to fellowship with you anyway? If you've ever asked even one of these questions, I pray this book will help you answer these and so many more.

The Bible is the story of God's love for His creation—you and me. How would you have come to know Him if God's Spirit had not placed a need for Him in your life in the first place? The need for a Savior? The need for forgiveness? A need for love?

None of us want to call ourselves needy. Most of us consider needs as unwanted enemies. But not God. Our Faithful Father knows that we can do nothing apart from His intervention. Yet we constantly try to meet the deepest needs of our lives on our own. Whether physically, mentally, emotionally, or spiritually, we encounter problems and challenges from the moment we are born.

Haven't we all experienced fear? Distress? Disappointment? Pain? Don't we all need encouragement? Peace? Comfort? Intimacy? Hope? Our needs line up like fence posts, trying to imprison us. But our Father's faithfulness knows no boundaries. He sees our needs differently because He created us. He knows how helpless we are without Him.

What if your needs were God's personal invitation to experience His faithfulness in a greater way? When we think about needs and desires, we often fail to realize that God already has the supply for all our needs—before we even recognize them or ask for help. And He *longs* to meet them for us. And even if we know we can't "fix" ourselves, which comes first, the need or the supply? Which do you think of first?

God wants you to look to Him as the Supplier of every need you will ever experience. He is not the provider of every selfish desire you may conceive. But He does want you to look to Him—and to trust Him for every need in your life.

The apostle Paul experienced God's faithfulness daily and affirmed it with confidence: *And my God will meet all your needs according to the riches of his glory in Christ Jesus* (Philippians 4:19 NIV).

The writer of Hebrews further testifies to God's faithful activity: *Let us then approach God's throne of grace with confidence, so that we may receive mercy and find grace to help us in our time of need* (Hebrews 4:16 NIV).

Our Faithful Father wants to meet our deepest needs, whether we classify the need simply as more of Him, or as a concern in critical areas of our lives on earth. He desires our intimacy when we're faithless, when we're scared, and when we're hurting. He wants us to understand His faithfulness when we're celebrating, when we're succeeding, and when we're confused. He's faithful not because He may answer our prayers favorably, or because He works things out eventually. He is faithful in His actions because He is faithful to His very name (s)—just because of who He is.

Why I Wrote This Book and How to Use It

Ever since writing *Daily in Your Presence, Intimate Conversations with a Loving Father,* and its sequel, *Daily in Your Image, Reflecting the Character of Christ*, almost 20 years ago, I've wanted to write another similar book about the faithfulness of God. However, I guess you could say I've been writing this book all my life, because to write about the faithfulness of God as I know it, is to include His entire activity in my life from birth to the present. And now 20 years later, I've learned so much more about God's precious, unchanging faithfulness.

With a team of consultants' help, I ultimately chose the same intimate conversation style in *Day-votions® with Your Faithful Father* as I used for *Daily in Your Presence* and *Daily in Your Image*. The *Day-votions®* trademark used in my three-book *Day-votions®* series for women has become the umbrella name for this and other future books.

Each chapter of *Day-votions® with Your Faithful Father* has longer prayers and additional content designed to deepen your devotional time and intimacy with God. You'll find not only a focal Scripture passage but also even more Bible verses to aid in your study.

I probably spent more time studying these verses than I did working on the actual prayer conversations. As I've studied the Bible through the years, I've tried to record the names, attributes, or activity of our faithful God. Those became the *supply*—and the basis for every intimate prayer conversation *From Your Faithful Father's Heart* in this book. They are like hidden treasures tucked into the pages of God's Word for me, ready to be discovered and experienced.

I searched every Bible verse in over twenty translations or versions before choosing the one that I felt communicated God's attribute or activity the best. I wanted to make sure the words chosen from my Faithful Father were sound, biblical, and accurate. I also used a commentary study of each passage to avoid pulling Scriptures out of context. If you don't see Bible verses that line up with your Faithful Father's conversations in a particular chapter, you will find the application in another. There simply wasn't room to include all the applicable verses in each chapter.

God is a triune God. I've approached these prayers from Him as a Faithful Father that way. The words in one prayer/chapter may be a reference to Jesus Himself as the Son of God, while in others, the words from God will talk about His Son or His Spirit. Jesus Himself said, "I and my Father are one" (John 10:30 KJV). Perhaps the Trinity—God in three persons—is a mystery we will understand only in heaven.

These prayers *From Your Faithful Father's Heart* are not words I've heard God speak to me audibly. I think of them as Rebecca's paraphrases, based on Scripture. I am not a biblical scholar. Any errors are my responsibility. But in teaching and studying the Bible for years, I have a simple love for Jesus and His Word. I've bathed this book in earnest prayer that God would use it to deepen your intimacy with Him. I'm still learning more about Him, and I hope I never stop. Will you commit with me to keep learning, searching, and drawing closer to God?

When you read the prayers *From Your Faithful Father's Heart*, I pray God's Spirit will speak to you in a way that will encourage, bless, and challenge you to spend more time in His Word, because God does speak to us. He may communicate through a friend, through His Word, through music, through His creation, and so many other ways. But His words and impressions will never contradict what He has already spoken in His Word.

It was not my intention to try to bring God down to our level or to lift us up to His. Through His grace and mercy, Jesus already did that.

When God spoke to ones like Job, Moses, Elijah, and others in the Bible, He often used questions. While Jesus lived on earth, He did the same thing, even answering a question with a question. These prayers *From Your Faithful Father's Heart* may do that as well, hopefully in a contemporary but biblically based way that will help you understand how faithful God is, and how much He loves you and wants to be involved in your life.

I hope the prayers offered *From a Grateful Heart* will both echo a need in your life and birth the gratitude God deserves from us—because He deserves our praise. Some of these prayers I wrote as if from my own heart; others were written as I would picture the faces of those who might be experiencing the needs.

By adding the extra material in *Daily Reflections* and *Daily Challenges*, you can use this book as either a personal or group Bible study. For a group study, simply divide the 90 chapters into several weeks, allowing the challenges to drive your discussion from the previous week's chapter readings. Use the *Daily Truth* as a takeaway to memorize or to solidify each chapter.

In the print book, you'll also find a place in each chapter for writing down your thoughts, prayers, and answers to the daily challenge, or simply reflections from each devotion. I added this feature because recording our thoughts are so important in remembering what we've read. And remembering God's goodness and faithfulness leads to a grateful heart. Use it as a guided journal to enhance your study and devotion to Him.

I've written this book primarily for those who already have a relationship with God through Jesus Christ. But if you know someone who has not yet made the wonderful discovery of knowing God and becoming His child, you can also use this book and the truths in it to introduce someone to Him for the first time.

If you are not yet a follower of Jesus, but you want to know more, please turn to *Begin the Journey* at the back of the book. There, you'll find help in making that decision.

As you spend 90 days with the One who wants to meet all your needs, I pray this book will help you discover our Father's amazing love and His unchanging faithfulness to you in a new, life-changing way, and that it will draw you even closer to Him.

-Rebecca

DAY 1

When You Need to Release the Past
The One Who Gives You a Fresh Start

*Great is his faithfulness;
his mercies begin afresh each morning.*
Lamentations 3:23 NLT

FROM YOUR FAITHFUL FATHER'S HEART

My child, are you focusing on past mistakes instead of My faithfulness to forgive? Have you forgotten all the sweet times of fellowship we've shared? I am still the One who gives you a fresh start. Am I not powerful enough to forgive your past and redesign your future? Relying only on human efforts can push you into habits and beliefs that harm you rather than move you forward. I want to help you see the new work I've designed for you. I will exchange your old dreams and patterns for My new ones because what I envision for you is far greater than anything you could ever imagine. Remember My grace, but release your painful past. I've already forgiven you. All I want is your complete trust in Me. In your spirit, the faith part of you that longs to move beyond your mistakes and your limited vision, you will sense My Spirit's stirring. Give yourself time, and wait on Me. I will complete the work I started in you.

FROM A GRATEFUL HEART

Lord, I look at my scars and remember the pain of my sinfulness. Some wounds are still healing. My enemy loves to remind me of my past. But then I remember Your scars—the true cost of my faithlessness. And in those marks, I see fresh mercies and grace from Your precious hands. If You opened the Red Sea, delivered Daniel from the lion's den, and raised people from the dead, You are powerful enough to give me a new start. I'm ready to abandon anything to experience Your best for me. I lay every fault, every fear, and every failure at Your feet. You are the One who gives me a fresh start. Give me new eyes of faith. Today I'm starting a new pattern of trusting in You. I desperately need a new beginning.

DAILY TRUTH
When Jesus steps in, new things begin.

DAILY REFLECTIONS
Therefore if any man be in Christ, he is a new creature: old things are passed away; behold, all things are become new. 2 Corinthians 5:17 KJV

And I am sure that God who began the good work within you will keep right on helping you grow in his grace until his task within you is finally finished on that day when Jesus Christ returns. Philippians 1:6 TLB

Faith shows the reality of what we hope for; it is the evidence of things we cannot see. Hebrews 11:1 NLT

"But forget all that—it is nothing compared to what I am going to do. For I am about to do something new. See, I have already begun! Do you not see it?" Isaiah 43:18-19 NLT

DAILY CHALLENGE
How do these verses motivate you to make a fresh start? Do you remember your scars as wounds from your past or as reminders of God's grace? What would happen if you decided to treat every day as if it were the first day of your life? That's the kind of grace opportunity Jesus offers us daily. Will you make a fresh start today?

DAILY THOUGHTS & PRAYERS

Day 2

When You Need Guidance
The One Who Keeps You On Track

Trust God from the bottom of your heart; don't try to figure out everything on your own. Listen for God's voice in everything you do, everywhere you go; he's the one who will keep you on track.
Proverbs 3:5-6 MSG

FROM YOUR FAITHFUL FATHER'S HEART
My child, have I ever left you on your own? Have I ever once left you all alone? Remember those frightening experiences as a child when you let go of your mother's hand and separated from her temporarily? Remember those occasions when you thought I had abandoned you? Maybe those were the times you released My hand. That absence of closeness you felt from Me could have been the distance you initiated. I was always there with you. I am still the One who keeps you on track. When you need guidance, don't look to the left or the right; just look at Me. I will lead you where I want you to go. I'll keep you from being derailed. I will give you strength for each day's journey. Be still, and you will hear My voice whispering to you through My Word, confirming your direction. Even if the way looks dark, I am your faithful Father who will still be with you, holding your hand, guiding your steps, and walking beside you all the way.

FROM A GRATEFUL HEART
Lord, I confess my failure to follow You, the times when I let go of Your hand and tried to find my own path. How did that work out for me? Painfully. Your Word says You and Your faithfulness will not fail. You cannot fail, because You never change. You will never leave me alone. Your faithfulness is like a flashlight in the dark. Day after day, You guide my faltering steps, prodding me to move with Your Spirit. Even when I try to figure out things on my own and choose the wrong way, You correct me and remind me of Your promises. I need Your guidance, Lord. I couldn't make it

without You. You are the One who keeps me on track. Why should I worry when Your presence is all around me? Why should I fear the future when You are leading me, one day at a time?

DAILY TRUTH
God has excellent night vision.

DAILY REFLECTIONS
Your own ears will hear him. Right behind you a voice will say, "This is the way you should go," whether to the right or to the left. Isaiah 30:21 NLT

Your word is a lamp for my feet, a light on my path. Psalm 119:105 NIV

For God has said, "I will never fail you. I will never abandon you." Hebrews 13:5 NLT

Our faith may fail, his never wanes—That's who he is, he cannot change! 2 Timothy 2:13 ISV

DAILY CHALLENGE
Have you ever felt like God abandoned you? Describe those feelings. How do these Scripture verses give you confidence and alleviate fear? The next time you need guidance, ask your faithful Father first. Spend time searching His Word and mark additional verses that promise His guidance and direction in your life. Instead of moving ahead on your own steam, wait and ask for His direction and strength.

DAILY THOUGHTS & PRAYERS

Day 3

When Disappointment Comes
The One Who Never Disappoints

"Those who believe in him will never be disappointed."
Romans 9:33 TLB

FROM YOUR FAITHFUL FATHER'S HEART
My child, disappointment can creep into your life like an unseen enemy. Just like in a marriage or a family, when you hold on to misplaced expectations, you will meet frustration head-on. Imperfect people will let you down; circumstances will cloud your perspective, and life will disappoint you. Sometimes you even get angry with Me if My answers are not what you expected or if I don't come through like you thought I would. But I will never withhold My love or anything good from My children. I am the One who never disappoints. And I always know what's best for you. How you choose to respond is up to you. But instead of giving up, try giving your discontentment to Me. Are you afraid that I will disappoint you if you place your life and circumstances in My hands? I've always been faithful. My Holy Spirit has flooded your heart with My love and security. When you open your heart to Me, placing your hopes and expectations in Me, I have promised you a wonderful love relationship with Me—the One who never disappoints.

FROM A GRATEFUL HEART
Lord, You've never been the source of my disappointment. I recognize my misplaced blame and the power of Your name and character. At times I've let my fear be a stumbling stone that keeps me from the joy and peace You've planned for me. I can so easily base my faith on past experiences: broken relationships, unfulfilled hopes, or unrealized dreams. Like so many, I ignore the truth, trusting instead in myself or others as if that will smooth my path and bring the needed answers I want. But that's not what I desire. I know You are the only way to a hope-filled life. If I stumble, let me

stumble into Your arms. You are the One who never disappoints, and You will never disappoint me.

DAILY TRUTH

Disappointment is only an appointment to trust God more.

DAILY REFLECTIONS

We need have no fear of someone who loves us perfectly; his perfect love for us eliminates all dread of what he might do to us. If we are afraid, it is for fear of what he might do to us and shows that we are not fully convinced that he really loves us. 1 John 4:18 TLB

And this hope will not lead to disappointment. For we know how dearly God loves us, because he has given us the Holy Spirit to fill our hearts with his love. Romans 5:5 NLT

I pray that God, the source of hope, will fill you completely with joy and peace because you trust in him. Then you will overflow with confident hope through the power of the Holy Spirit. Romans 15:13 NLT

Lord, when doubts fill my mind, when my heart is in turmoil, quiet me and give me renewed hope and cheer. Psalm 94:19 TLB

DAILY CHALLENGE

After reading these Scriptures, write down any recent disappointments you've experienced. How did you react? Do you see any misplaced expectations? One by one, turn them over to God and ask Him to renew your life with joy. How would you like to respond to disappointments the next time you encounter them?

DAILY THOUGHTS & PRAYERS

Day 4

When You Long to Make God Happy
The One Who Takes Pleasure in You

*When you give them your breath, life is created,
and you renew the face of the earth.
May the glory of the LORD continue forever!
The LORD takes pleasure in all he has made!*
Psalm 104:30-31 NLT

FROM YOUR FAITHFUL FATHER'S HEART
My child, did you know you make Me smile? Just visualizing your life before you were born, and then hearing your first cry at birth gave Me great pleasure. Like a father and child, our relationship grows stronger as you seek Me daily. I created you in My image for intimate fellowship and for My glory. I am nurturing you with My love. There is nothing you can do to change My feelings for you. When you belong to Me, you live in My light and experience the joy I've always planned for you. Your choice to follow Me with all your heart and to acknowledge Me as Lord of your life brings us into a sweet communion. That fellowship can only be broken when you fail temporarily to put Me first in your life. I am the One who takes pleasure in you. Our relationship is secure. I'm proud to call you "My child."

FROM A GRATEFUL HEART
Lord, I am constantly amazed at the way You feel about me. No matter what I do, You keep on loving me. Your love is always perfect. I don't need to prove anything to You or try to impress You in any way. I love You, Lord, just because! Because You first loved me and gave Your Son's life for me. You could have loved me without making me Your child. But You chose through Jesus' death and resurrection to offer me that gift. To know that I make You happy just being Your child makes me want to do more—so much more for You. You are the One who takes pleasure in me and all Your children. Thank You, Lord!

DAILY TRUTH
The greatest treasure and the sweetest pleasure we will ever know is our love relationship with Jesus.

DAILY REFLECTIONS
Long before he laid down earth's foundations, he had us in mind, had settled on us as the focus of his love, to be made whole and holy by his love. Long, long ago he decided to adopt us into his family through Jesus Christ. (What pleasure he took in planning this!) He wanted us to enter into the celebration of his lavish gift-giving by the hand of his beloved Son. Ephesians 1:4-6 MSG

But if we are living in the light of God's presence, just as Christ does, then we have wonderful fellowship and joy with each other, and the blood of Jesus his Son cleanses us from every sin. 1 John 1:7 TLB

For the Lord takes pleasure in His people. Psalm 149:4 NKJV

See how very much our Father loves us, for he calls us his children, and that is what we are! 1 John 3:1 NLT

DAILY CHALLENGE
Ask God to reveal any ways you've tried to please Him through self-efforts, consciously or unconsciously. Then every morning as you look in the mirror, thank Him that He loves you just as you are. Write "I love You, Lord, because," and list as many reasons as you can why you love your faithful Father.

DAILY THOUGHTS & PRAYERS

Day 5

When You Need Encouragement
The One Who Encourages the Discouraged

*When we arrived in Macedonia, there was no rest for us.
We faced conflict from every direction, with battles on the outside and fear
on the inside. But God, who encourages those who are discouraged,
encouraged us by the arrival of Titus.*
2 Corinthians 7:5-6 NLT

FROM YOUR FAITHFUL FATHER'S HEART
My child, are you discouraged? Has life saddened you or frustrated your desires? Are you struggling with the tension between right and wrong? All My children will be tempted with discouragement when situations turn sour. But you can choose a different response. In this world, you will always experience conflict, but I will bring you peace and encouragement even in your turmoil. I will inspire you with courage and confidence to push through your troubles. I have overcome the world through My victory on the cross. Because of your relationship with Me, you can rise above those things that threaten to deter or dishearten you. Whether I whisper a familiar promise or send a friend to help bear your burdens, remember I am still the One who encourages the discouraged. In Me, you will find peace and hope.

FROM A GRATEFUL HEART
Lord, conflict is like a nagging north wind always blowing in at just the wrong time. I withdraw to find warmth, only to discover the heater is broken inside. Yet when I stop and look up, You remind me that You are the One who encourages the discouraged. Time and time again, You have ministered to me through Your appointed earth angels, friends who have stepped in just when I needed them most. Other times, I open Your Word or utter a cry, and You are there, always ready to help. Your constant presence warms my spirit. You not only help me to overcome my weaknesses;

You also give me the strength to move forward. Thank You, Lord, for Your encouraging words and perfect timing.

DAILY TRUTH
When God encourages us, He sends courage into us.

DAILY REFLECTIONS
"I have told you these things, so that in me you may have peace. In this world you will have trouble. But take heart! I have overcome the world." John 16:33 NIV

May our Lord Jesus Christ himself and God our Father, who loved us and by his grace gave us eternal encouragement and good hope, encourage your hearts and strengthen you in every good deed and word. 2 Thessalonians 2:16-17 NIV

"Have I not commanded you? Be strong and courageous. Do not be afraid; do not be discouraged, for the LORD your God will be with you wherever you go." Joshua 1:9 NIV

Therefore encourage one another and build each other up. 1 Thessalonians 5:11 NIV

DAILY CHALLENGE
If discouragement tries to sneak into your life, stop and examine its roots. What or who has caused you to feel weak or discouraged? Memorize Joshua 1:9 and think of ways God has encouraged you. If it helps, write down a few of those experiences. Call a close Christian friend if you need extra encouragement during rough times.

DAILY THOUGHTS & PRAYERS

Day 6

When Your Heart Needs a Home
The One Who Makes You Family

*Now you are no longer strangers to God and foreigners to heaven,
but you are members of God's very own family,
citizens of God's country, and you belong in God's household
with every other Christian.*
Ephesians 2:19 TLB

FROM YOUR FAITHFUL FATHER'S HEART

My child, are you feeling lonely? Do you long for a place to call home? You are not alone in this world. And if you truly know Me, you never will be, because I am always with you. Not only have I made a home in your heart; I have given you a home in Mine. You are a part of My forever family. Your relationships on earth are limited. Even if you tracked down all your ancestors, the number couldn't compare to your spiritual family. Through My Spirit, you've gained brothers and sisters around the world. You were once an alien and a stranger, but now your roots grow deep into My love. I required no payment from you for your citizenship in heaven. I paid for it with My death so you could join My household by faith. I dissolved the enmity of hatred and provided a way for unity, love, and peace. Spread the word, My child. I am the One who makes you family, and I want everyone to belong.

FROM A GRATEFUL HEART

Lord, thank You for accepting me and making me part of Your family. Knowing that I am at home in Your heart gives me great joy. The relationship I share with You is like no other. How grateful I am that You tore down the barriers so all could come to know You. When we receive You by faith, You are the One who makes us all family. Yet the choice is ours. Will we choose to become Your children? I'm so glad I did. I pray for my brothers and sisters in Christ and for the ones I've never met. May we all honor

You as our true, faithful Father. Together with all Your children, we can form the body of Christ, bonded in love, dedicated to making Your name known, so that all can experience the true joy of family.

DAILY TRUTH
Only in Christ can we truly know the bonds of love.

DAILY REFLECTIONS
I pray that from his glorious, unlimited resources he will empower you with inner strength through his Spirit. Then Christ will make his home in your hearts as you trust in him. Your roots will grow down into God's love and keep you strong. Ephesians 3:16-17 NLT

He makes a home for those who are alone. Psalm 68:6 VOICE

He is the embodiment of our peace, sent once and for all to take down the great barrier of hatred and hostility that has divided us so that we can be one. Ephesians 2:14 VOICE

You have been bought and paid for by Christ, so you belong to him. 1 Corinthians 7:23 TLB

DAILY CHALLENGE
Draw a large heart representing God's heart. Add a tiny heart in the middle to represent you. Fill in the rest of the space with small hearts to symbolize a fraction of your spiritual family—other believers from around the world. Write down a few familiar names from your spiritual family and pray for them this week. Praying Ephesians 3:16-17 for them is a good place to start. Thank God daily that you belong to Him.

DAILY THOUGHTS & PRAYERS

Day 7

When You Wonder If God Really Loves You
The One Who Loves the Entire World

For God so loved the world that he gave his one and only Son,
that whoever believes in him
shall not perish but have eternal life.
John 3:16 NIV

FROM YOUR FAITHFUL FATHER'S HEART

My child, do you know how much I really love you? Have you questioned My heart at times? Most people gauge love by their emotions. But My love reflects My character. I don't love you one day and then hate you the next. My love mirrors My faithful commitment to you. How much do I love you? How much do I love the entire world? I went to great lengths to prove My unchangeable love for you, to convince you that I wanted you as My child. I sent My one and only Son to earth with an eternal message, indelibly written with His blood on a splintered cross. He bore your sins and provided your healing. I will always be the One who loves you and the entire world. My Son gave His life for your life—for the whole world. Nail-scarred hands, opened wide, every cry of agony echoed: "I did it for you!"

FROM A GRATEFUL HEART

Lord, I confess I've doubted Your love at times. I've interpreted circumstances in light of my perspective and allowed emotions to run wild like a roller coaster. But when my heart and head clear, I can truly declare that I've never known a faithful love like Yours. Your actions defy all understanding. I can't explain it. I can't define it. But I do accept it. And I'm only one person. Jesus died for the whole world—for all of Your creation. We've all turned away from You and gone our own way, Lord. None of us are worthy of Your love. Yet even in our worst moments, Your love never wavers. Thank You for sending Jesus. We are the ones who deserved death, not Your own Son. You are the One who loves me and the entire world. Thank

You, Lord, for loving me unconditionally.

DAILY TRUTH
Love first began with God.

DAILY REFLECTIONS
All of us, like sheep, have strayed away. We have left God's paths to follow our own. Yet the LORD laid on him the sins of us all. Isaiah 53:6 NLT

For when the time was right, the Anointed One came and died to demonstrate his love for sinners who were entirely helpless, weak, and powerless to save themselves. Now, would anyone dare to die for the sake of a wicked person? We can all understand if someone was willing to die for a truly noble person. But Christ proved God's passionate love for us by dying in our place while we were still lost and ungodly! Romans 5:6-8 TPT

Your unfailing love is better than life itself; how I praise you! Psalm 63:3 NLT

This is how we know what love is: Jesus Christ laid down his life for us. 1 John 3:16 NIV

DAILY CHALLENGE
After studying these Scripture verses, write down as many adjectives as you can think of to describe God's love for you. On another sheet of paper, draw a picture of a cross and post it on your refrigerator or a place where you will see it often to remind you how much God loves you.

DAILY THOUGHTS & PRAYERS

Day 8

When You Don't Know What to Do
The One Who Teaches You What Is Good for You

*"I am the Lord your God,
who teaches you what is good for you
and leads you along the paths you should follow."*
Isaiah 48:17 NLT

FROM YOUR FAITHFUL FATHER'S HEART
My child, have I ever failed to do what I promised? Have I ever withheld My wisdom from you when you asked? I am still the faithful One who teaches you what is good for you. You don't need to panic and wring your hands, wondering what to do. Worry will only block your creativity and push you to find solutions on your own. I am only a prayer away, as I wait for your willing submission. When you don't know what to do, keep your eyes on Me. Be patient, and rest while you wait for Me. When you ask for wisdom, don't doubt Me or My response. I may delay an answer, and I may answer differently than what you expect. My paths may even lead you in an unfamiliar direction. But My ways are far better than you can ever imagine. I simply want your obedience and for you to trust Me with your whole heart, not just a part. When you seek Me first, I will always lead you in the right direction.

FROM A GRATEFUL HEART
Lord, how many times You would have blessed me if only I had listened and waited for Your instructions. Sometimes I thought I knew the right path to follow, so I stubbornly ran the opposite direction and failed to heed Your warnings. I'm so thankful for Your grace and for not giving up on me. Thank You for being the One who teaches me what is good for me. I want to follow Your leadership. Help me, Lord, to say "Yes," when You call. When I don't know what to do, I will focus on You, and I will keep listening. Your paths and Your ways are always best. Today, my heart cries out in

submission to You, Lord. Where You lead, I will follow.

DAILY TRUTH
Rocky paths with Jesus are safer than smooth ones on my own.

DAILY REFLECTIONS
Trust in the LORD with all your heart; do not depend on your own understanding. Seek his will in all you do, and he will show you which path to take. Proverbs 3:5-6 NLT

"We do not know what to do, but our eyes are on you."
2 Chronicles 20:12 NIV

Be still in the presence of the LORD, and wait patiently for him to act. Psalm 37:7 NLT

If any of you needs wisdom to know what you should do, you should ask God, and he will give it to you. God is generous to everyone and doesn't find fault with them. When you ask for something, don't have any doubts. A person who has doubts is like a wave that is blown by the wind and tossed by the sea. James 1:5-6 GW

DAILY CHALLENGE
Read 2 Chronicles 20:1-20. What was King Jehoshaphat's prayer to God when an enemy army declared war on his nation? Have you experienced any situations where you have uttered this prayer? Record your thoughts. Memorize Proverbs 3:5-6 and place that verse beside your mirror or desk. Each morning, make that Bible verse a part of your prayer to God for the day.

DAILY THOUGHTS & PRAYERS

Day 9

When You Need to Find Your Purpose
The One Who Made You for His Glory

*"Bring all who claim me as their God,
for I have made them for my glory. It was I who created them."*
Isaiah 43:7 NLT

FROM YOUR FAITHFUL FATHER'S HEART

My child, do you struggle with your purpose in life? I hear your questions: "Why did God make me? For great success? Grand adventures? Monastery solitude?" At the end of the day, your earthly resume may read, "ordinary" or "unremarkable." Do you think that matters to Me? Your universal purpose is not so difficult to understand. I am the One who made you for My glory. I created you because I wanted to. I love you, and your purpose is to reflect My glory in all you do, using My unique blueprint for your life. I designed your skills and abilities and have given you spiritual gifts to help encourage and build up My Church, the body of Christ. Whatever you choose to do, when you desire to honor Me, and your purpose and activities bring Me glory, that makes Me smile.

FROM A GRATEFUL HEART

Lord, sometimes I complicate life by asking unnecessary questions. "Is my name on this? Am I on the right path? What is my purpose, anyway? What if I'm not successful in what You called me to do?" And then I hear Your sweet whispers through the pages of Scripture. You are the One who made me for Your glory, not mine. Not so I could achieve a place in the Guinness Book of World Records or attain great worldly success. You created me for Yourself. My life brings pleasure to You because I am Your child. I can enjoy whatever task You set before me because You have gifted me uniquely and given me a desire to honor You. No matter where You place me, help me bring glory to You alone, so I can point others to You.

DAILY TRUTH
God loves for us to bring Him glory by sharing His love story, everywhere we go.

DAILY REFLECTIONS
Now may the God of peace—who brought up from the dead our Lord Jesus, the great Shepherd of the sheep, and ratified an eternal covenant with his blood—may he equip you with all you need for doing his will. Hebrews 13:20-21 NLT

Whatever you do, do it all for the glory of God. 1 Corinthians 10:31 NLT

And we know that God causes everything to work together for the good of those who love God and are called according to his purpose for them. Romans 8:28 NLT

For it is [not your strength, but it is] God who is effectively at work in you, both to will and to work [that is, strengthening, energizing, and creating in you the longing and the ability to fulfill your purpose] for His good pleasure. Philippians 2:13 AMP

DAILY CHALLENGE
Write down the natural skills and abilities God has given you. Read 1 Corinthians 12, Romans 12:3-13; Ephesians 4:1-16, and 1 Peter 4:10-11 to learn more about God's spiritual gifts. What gives you the most pleasure when serving God and others? In what area of service or spiritual gifting do you find a minimum of weariness and a maximum of joy?

DAILY THOUGHTS & PRAYERS

Day 10

When You're Tired of Trying
The One Who Never Grows Tired or Weary

*Do you not know? Have you not heard?
The Lord is the everlasting God,
the Creator of the ends of the earth.
He will not grow tired or weary,
and his understanding no one can fathom.*
Isaiah 40:28 NIV

FROM YOUR FAITHFUL FATHER'S HEART
My child, are you struggling with a lack of energy? Your spirit says, "Yes!" but your body cries, "No way!" Are you carrying burdens never intended for you? I am sufficient for every task. I will give you the power you need to keep going. I am the One who never grows tired or weary. I know your limitations. But I also promise that My strength will be yours. Not only will I give you rest when you wait on Me; but I will also recharge your batteries, refresh your body and spirit, and renew your passion to stay in the race. Some days you will feel tired—tired of trying, running, or falling. Tired of struggling to keep up. Those are the times you especially need Me. As you cast all your cares, weariness, and weaknesses on Me, I will overhaul your body, mind, and spirit. I will breathe new life into you if you will only ask.

FROM A GRATEFUL HEART
Lord, I'm so tired of trying to do things on my own. Some days I feel like a hurricane-battered home, reduced to a sagging frame. I'm eager to complete the journey You designed for me. But I can't do it by myself, and I have nothing left to give. Today I'm laying my worries and burdens at Your feet. I believe that You will help me soar like an eagle when I wait on You. Instead of running away, I will run to You for fresh grace to complete my race with courage and stamina. Thank You, Lord, that You are the One who never grows tired or weary. Because of the faithful Father You are, You

know what I need, even before I ask. Your grace is sufficient and always available. Only in You can I find the strength to continue.

DAILY TRUTH
God's strength is the perfect RX for our weariness.

DAILY REFLECTIONS
But those who wait for the LORD [who expect, look for, and hope in Him] Will gain new strength and renew their power; They will lift up their wings [and rise up close to God] like eagles [rising toward the sun]; They will run and not become weary, They will walk and not grow tired. Isaiah 40:31 AMP

So here's what I've learned through it all: Leave all your cares and anxieties at the feet of the Lord, and measureless grace will strengthen you. Psalm 55:22 TPT

Look to the LORD and his strength; seek his face always. Psalm 105:4 NIV

But he said to me, "My grace is sufficient for you, for my power is made perfect in weakness." 2 Corinthians 12:9 NIV

DAILY CHALLENGE
Meditate on these verses and Matthew 11:28. If you are not accustomed to taking a Sabbath rest—one day a week to increase your focus on God, praying, worshipping, and reading His Word, and time away from strenuous work—do so this week. Gather with other worshippers honoring God as well. If possible, increase your amount of sleep each night. And if necessary, take an occasional nap.

DAILY THOUGHTS & PRAYERS

Day 11

When Fear Closes In
The One Who Comforts You

*"I, I'm the One comforting you.
What are you afraid of—or who?"*
Isaiah 51:12 MSG

FROM YOUR FAITHFUL FATHER'S HEART
My child, why are you afraid? Are you turning to others or Me for reassurance in times of trouble and distress? You look around and see danger and disaster. In those dark moments when fear stalks you and whispers irrational thoughts, remember My words and promises. Have you forgotten that I am the One who comforts you? I give peace, not fear or confusion. What can anyone do to you when I am holding you securely? When in doubt, I want you to faith it out and trust Me. My arms are big enough to hold you. My heart is tender enough to understand your fears. And My comfort is so real You can sense My breath upon your spirit whispering sweet peace to your soul. You only need to fear Me. That doesn't mean being afraid of Me. For My children, that means reverencing Me, respecting Me, and acknowledging Me as your faithful Father. Love for you is always behind My plans, My actions, and My activities.

FROM A GRATEFUL HEART
Lord, refill the holes that fear has ravaged. When irrational fears try to suffocate me, Your presence is near. Your right arm, like an eagle's wing, spreads out over my heart, my life, and my spirit, and shields me from my enemies who try to sway my faith and reduce me to a coward. At times I don't understand the trials or the trouble You allow me to experience. But when they pass, and I'm still standing, I realize part of their purpose: to make me strong, and to help me comfort others in the same way You have comforted me. Dark valleys will not block out the Son in my life. Your Spirit accompanies me on my journey, and Your comfort never leaves. You are

indeed the One who comforts me. Thank You that You will deliver me from all my phobias. With You in my life, I never need to be afraid.

DAILY TRUTH
God's comfort is a cloak we can wear daily.

DAILY REFLECTIONS
"Because he loves me," says the Lord, "I will rescue him; I will protect him, for he acknowledges my name." Psalm 91:14 NIV

I cling to you; your strong right hand holds me securely. Psalm 63:8 NLT

I prayed to the Lord, and he answered me. He freed me from all my fears. Psalm 34:4 NLT

All praise to God, the Father of our Lord Jesus Christ. God is our merciful Father and the source of all comfort. He comforts us in all our troubles so that we can comfort others. When they are troubled, we will be able to give them the same comfort God has given us. 2 Corinthians 1:3-4 NLT

DAILY CHALLENGE
After reading these Scripture verses, make a list of any irrational fears and ask God to deliver you from them. Grab a soft blanket and drape it over your shoulders. Close your eyes and picture Jesus wrapping His strong arms around you. Thank Him for His daily comfort. For further help, search for other Bible verses and promises about fear. Keep a list of those references handy to remember each time fear tries to find an entrance.

DAILY THOUGHTS & PRAYERS

Day 12

When Your God Isn't Big Enough
The One Who Can Do Anything

*"I am the Lord, the God of all mankind.
Is anything too hard for me?"*
Jeremiah 32:27 NIV

FROM YOUR FAITHFUL FATHER'S HEART
My child, how do you envision Me? As a tyrant who rules with an iron fist? As a kindly, aged grandfather who winks at wrong, too weak to interfere with your life? Do you think I'm a distant CEO who has no time for the common laborer? A confused scientist who can't control his creation? I am none of those things. However you define Me, your description will never be big enough. And it will never be completely accurate. I am still the One who can do anything. Your finite mind wants to understand Me, explain My nature, and believe who I say I am. But you can only embrace the great *I Am* by faith. I want you to see Me bigger, to magnify My name, My character, and all that I am. I want you to know that all things are possible when I speak the word. I can shake the earth from its axis. One word from Me could destroy all My creation. But I also mend broken hearts, give sight to the blind, and free prisoners from patterns of sin. I stretched the heavens like a canopy for billions of lights, and I can expand your heart to embrace My love. I want only good for you. With Me, anything is possible. Only believe, My child. Only believe.

FROM A GRATEFUL HEART
Lord God, enlarge my faith and my vision of who You really are. You give me opportunities daily to witness Your miracles. Yet sometimes I miss them. I try to make things happen instead of watching, praying, and depending on You for the deepest needs of my heart. Are You still the One who flung the stars into space, hollowed out mountains and valleys, and formed man from the dust of the earth, breathing life into him? Is that

God limited in any way? Oh, God! Open the eyes of my heart and spirit to embrace the magnificence of who You are. You are indeed an awesome God. You are the One who can do anything. Help me see. Help me believe.

DAILY TRUTH
Our belief doesn't enable God; it enables us to participate in who He is.

DAILY REFLECTIONS
Oh, magnify the Lord with me, And let us exalt His name together. Psalm 34:3 NKJV

God said to Moses, "I am who I am." Exodus 3:14 NIV

"I know that you can do anything, and no one can stop you." Job 42:2 NLT

Christ himself is the Creator who made everything in heaven and earth, the things we can see and the things we can't; the spirit world with its kings and kingdoms, its rulers and authorities; all were made by Christ for his own use and glory. Colossians 1:16 TLB

DAILY CHALLENGE
In what ways have you ever made God too small? Is there anything you think God can't do? As you study His Word daily, begin a list of His attributes and characteristics. How do those words help magnify who God is for you? How do they help you "see" Him bigger? Is there something you are asking your faithful Father to do? Include that in your list. Will you trust Him for that today?

DAILY THOUGHTS & PRAYERS

Day 13

When You Want to Help Others Change
The One Who Changes Lives

*This same Good News that came to you is going out all over the world. It is bearing fruit everywhere by changing lives,
just as it changed your lives from the day you first heard
and understood the truth about God's wonderful grace.*
Colossians 1:6 NLT

FROM YOUR FAITHFUL FATHER'S HEART
My child, I know your temptation to play God. Do you remember what your life was like before you met Me? Could you change yourself? Do you understand more about My grace now than you did then? Keep sharing the truth and the good news that first changed you. You may not always see the fruits of your labor immediately, but as you obediently live, rooted in Me, My life will flow through you, and others will see the changes in you. You will reap a blessing in My time, so never stop believing. Remember that no one can come to Me except My faithful Father draws them. They must choose to respond to Me. My Spirit is always working behind the scenes. Pray for others, and allow them to see My great love through you. You do the loving; I will do the changing. I am still the One who changes lives. And I will lose none that my Father has given to Me. They will all join Me in heaven one day.

FROM A GRATEFUL HEART
Lord, I've tried unsuccessfully to change people. My desires are right but my methods are wrong. Sometimes I end up criticizing instead of comforting, or hurting instead of helping. Those are the times You show me I'm the one who needs changing. Your grace is amazing, and the good news is powerful, but You are the One who changes lives, not me. You are the One who brings repentance. Trying to convince people on my own doesn't work. It's Your Spirit that draws people into a relationship with You. Thank

You for constantly working in my life. I will continue to love others and to share Your good news, Lord. What wonderful news it is!

DAILY TRUTH
God is the Life-bringer and the Life-changer.

DAILY REFLECTIONS
So let's not get tired of doing what is good. At just the right time we will reap a harvest of blessing if we don't give up. Galatians 6:9 NLT

"No one can come to me unless the Father who sent me draws them, and I will raise them up at the last day." John 6:44 NIV

"And this is the will of him who sent me, that I shall lose none of all those he has given me, but raise them up at the last day." John 6:39 NIV

"I am the vine; you are the branches. If you remain in me and I in you, you will bear much fruit; apart from me you can do nothing." John 15:5 NIV

DAILY CHALLENGE
Write down your salvation experience in a few sentences. How did you become a follower of Christ? Who or what influenced you? In another sentence or two, add what God is doing in your life today. How has He made a difference in your life since you first came to know Him? Ask God to remind you of others who need His life-changing power. Place those names on a strip of paper in your Bible, on your journal pages, or list them on your cell phone. Pray for those people each day for 90 days.

DAILY THOUGHTS & PRAYERS

Day 14

When You Wonder About Your Worth
The One Who Calls You Priceless

"You are priceless to me. I love you and honor you."
Isaiah 43:4 NIrV

FROM YOUR FAITHFUL FATHER'S HEART
My child, I see you struggling at times, wondering if I really care about you. Your self-worth can plummet on any day, depending on where you look for validation. But just like a famous painting garners its value because of the artist's signature, remember that all My children are created uniquely by the Master Artist of the universe. I paid for you with My death, and that makes you priceless to Me. You are valuable to Me because I have signed My name in blood in your very DNA. The way I feel about you is not based on your performance. No, I love you—really love you—just because you are My child. I chose you, formed you, and loved you from the beginning. When you choose Me by faith and accept the gift of worth I offer you, something beautiful happens. Your beauty begins to emerge from the inside out. And that's when you'll want everything you do to really matter to Me, the One who calls you priceless.

FROM A GRATEFUL HEART
Lord, I can't begin to thank You enough for loving me just as I am. Forgive me for validating my life with social media "likes," by others' opinions, or by my daily accomplishments—or lack of them. I don't need to impress You or anyone else. I understand the price You paid for me, even when I was not worth loving. My life looked like an ordinary preschooler's scrawls until You took Your Master Artist's palette and added Your touch. From the blood You shed, You painted hope and life and left Your signature on the canvas of my soul. Help me to see myself as You see me: a work of Your heart, a true Artist's masterpiece. Thank You for giving me value and for the assurance that I am priceless to You.

DAILY TRUTH
You are a true work of art—created from God's own heart.

DAILY REFLECTIONS
But God showed his great love for us by sending Christ to die for us while we were still sinners. Romans 5:8 NLT

I will offer You my grateful heart, for I am Your unique creation, filled with wonder and awe. You have approached even the smallest details with excellence; Your works are wonderful; I carry this knowledge deep within my soul. Psalm 139:14 VOICE

For it's by God's grace that you have been saved. You receive it through faith. It was not our plan or our effort. It is God's gift, pure and simple. You didn't earn it, not one of us did, so don't go around bragging that you must have done something amazing. Ephesians 2:8-9 VOICE

Christ has paid the price for you. 1 Corinthians 6:20 NIrV

DAILY CHALLENGE
How much do you know about art? Do you know any artists? Do an online search for some famous "priceless" paintings. List a few well-known artists' names. What makes their paintings so expensive? According to these Bible verses, how does your faithful Father evaluate your worth? How does that make you feel? Thank God that His signature on your life determines that your value and your life are priceless.

DAILY THOUGHTS & PRAYERS

Day 15

When You Long for Deeper Intimacy with God
The One Who Satisfies You Completely

> *"Why do you spend money for what is not bread,*
> *And your wages for what does not satisfy?*
> *Listen carefully to Me, and eat what is good,*
> *And let your soul delight itself in abundance."*
> Isaiah 55:2 NKJV

FROM YOUR FAITHFUL FATHER'S HEART

My child, you enjoy all kinds of food and activities that leave you temporarily satisfied. But do you long for Me and the nourishment you need for your spiritual life? I am the One who satisfies you completely. At My banquet table, you can eat to your heart's content, any time you wish. You can waste your time and money on things that never satisfy you, or you can sit down in My presence and relish the food I've prepared for you. Listen to My words daily as you open the Bible and read. Taste, and see if what My Word says is true. I will give you the strength you need to face every trying situation. Every day I want to fill you with delicious delicacies—heavenly food that nourishes you. My food adds calories to your soul, giving you protection from sin-sickness and temptation. Why would you look for other things to satisfy when I'm all you need? Come, child. I'm waiting for you.

FROM A GRATEFUL HEART

Lord, too often I choose to run on empty, forgetting that You have prepared everything my body and soul need for life. I long for Your presence and Your life-giving food. Come and feed my soul. I'm so hungry for You. I know Your meals are perfectly planned and nutritious. Making Your words and provision my spiritual diet, I'm looking to You for complete satisfaction. Your words are a perfect five-course meal: appetizer, salad, soup, main course, and dessert, all rolled into one. You are life to me! I long to know You more fully, to draw closer to You, and to experience the deep intimacy with You for which I was created. No one can fill me like You, Lord. You are the One who satisfies me completely.

DAILY TRUTH
With God's food, you can count blessings, not calories.

DAILY REFLECTIONS
Taste and see that the Lord is good; blessed is the one who takes refuge in him. Psalm 34:8 NIV

You prepare a feast for me in the presence of my enemies. Psalm 23:5 NLT

"The Lord will guide you continually, And satisfy your soul in drought, And strengthen your bones." Isaiah 58:11 NKJV

I have hidden your word in my heart that I might not sin against you. Psalm 119:11 NIV

DAILY CHALLENGE
If you haven't already done so, select a time each day when you can indulge in a spiritual meal. You can make this book part of your five-course menu, adding prayers and notes. But you can also add a systematic read through the Bible, a chapter or two at a time, or let God's Spirit direct you to a passage you'll study each day. You can make notes beside any verses or subjects you'd like to use for your own personal Bible study. Then with a pen and notebook or journal, spend a few moments each day with God reading, praying, and recording what He shows you in His Word. Whatever plan you use, don't just snack. Eat heartily!

DAILY THOUGHTS & PRAYERS

Day 16

When God Seems Distant
The One Who Is Never Far from You

*"His purpose was for the nations to seek after God
and perhaps feel their way toward him and find him—
though he is not far from any one of us."*
Acts 17:27 NLT

FROM YOUR FAITHFUL FATHER'S HEART

My child, in this world, friends may let you down at a crucial time in your life. Those experiences can leave your heart disturbed, maybe even disillusioned. Sometimes you put Me in that same category. Do I seem far away? I want everyone to find Me, know Me, and love Me and to experience My glorious presence. I'm not a distant force somewhere who chooses un-involvement and separation from My creation. I want you to experience My presence and to discover My faithfulness in all things. I'm still the One who is always waiting nearby, the One who is never far from you. When you draw near to Me in submission, You will sense Me drawing close to you. Never be afraid to call on Me, especially in times of trouble or distress. Just as I protected My Son on earth, I will protect you from your enemy's darts. You never need to ask Me, "Where are You?" I'm never far from you, and as a follower of Christ, you have My Spirit living inside of you. It was My plan all along for you to experience joy, freedom, and blessing. Those who truly seek Me will always find Me waiting.

FROM A GRATEFUL HEART

Lord, in times of oppression when the walls have tried to close in on me, You've seemed so far away. Days passed. Silence lingered, except for the voices of my enemies' taunts that only grew louder. Then I stopped and looked up. I am so glad You are the One who is never far from me. The distance I may feel at times is because I have temporarily lost my way, or because my focus is not on You and Your faithfulness. My heart cries for

You daily: to know You, to love You, to serve You. Thank You for being near. You always hear my call and meet the deepest needs of my heart. I want both to guard and to share the precious treasures You have given me: the joy of Your salvation and Your faithful nearness and fellowship.

DAILY TRUTH
Seeking after God is always a win-win situation.

DAILY REFLECTIONS
"You will seek me and find me when you seek me with all your heart. I will be found by you," declares the Lord. Jeremiah 29:13-14 NIV

And when you draw close to God, God will draw close to you. James 4:8 TLB

"I will answer your cry for help every time you pray, and you will feel my presence in your time of trouble." Psalm 91:15 TPT

Through the power of the Holy Spirit who lives within us, carefully guard the precious truth that has been entrusted to you. 2 Timothy 1:14 NLT

DAILY CHALLENGE
Think about your friendships. What do you enjoy most about them? Has a friend ever let you down? What was that like? How did you respond? Has God ever felt distant to you? How do these verses assure you of God's nearness? Compare God's track record of faithfulness to your friends' loyalty. What do these verses tell you about God and His desire for intimacy with you? In what ways do you want to draw closer to your faithful Father?

DAILY THOUGHTS AND PRAYERS

Day 17

When Suffering Comes
The One Who Shares Your Suffering

*Through suffering,
our bodies continue to share in the death of Jesus
so that the life of Jesus may also be seen in our bodies.*
2 Corinthians 4:10 NLT

FROM YOUR FAITHFUL FATHER'S HEART

My child, you've questioned Me about pain and suffering in this world. No one likes to suffer. But you also live in a fallen world. Remember to treat trials and difficulties as friends that test and purify your faith, not as unpleasant interruptions, or even as enemies of your plans. Adam and Eve first experienced perfect fellowship with Me as their Creator, but their disobedience caused suffering. When persecution or turmoil threatens you, you can share in both My life and death. Never forget the unjust, undeserved sacrifice I endured for you. Can you see My love written in red? Suffering will come. It will not be the same for every child of Mine. But as the One who shares your suffering, I will walk with you through it. And when it is complete, your faith will emerge as pure gold.

FROM A GRATEFUL HEART

Lord, I am not a fan of suffering. Is anyone? All around me I see hurt, sorrow, and misery. I feel so helpless when others experience grief. And I don't always understand my own. Help me to see pain and persecution through Your eyes. Like a refiner's fire that removes impurities from metal, You will use these as instruments so You can shine brighter in us. Thank You for being the One who shares my suffering. Make me bold to live like Christ and never fear death. I have a long way to go. In this world, we will experience suffering, but You, Lord, will bring ultimate healing and victory to those who love You.

DAILY TRUTH
To be like Jesus may require more than our hearts are willing to give.

DAILY REFLECTIONS
Don't run from tests and hardships, brothers and sisters. As difficult as they are, you will ultimately find joy in them; if you embrace them, your faith will blossom under pressure and teach you true patience as you endure. And true patience brought on by endurance will equip you to complete the long journey and cross the finish line—mature, complete, and wanting nothing. James 1:2-4 VOICE

Adam's one sin brought the penalty of death to many, while Christ freely takes away many sins and gives glorious life instead. Romans 5:16 TLB

He said to God, "My Father, if there is not a way that you can deliver me from this suffering, then your will must be done." Matthew 26:42 TPT

Pure gold put in the fire comes out of it proved pure; genuine faith put through this suffering comes out proved genuine. When Jesus wraps this all up, it's your faith, not your gold, that God will have on display as evidence of his victory. 1 Peter 1:7 MSG

DAILY CHALLENGE
Do you wear a gold or silver ring with a precious stone? Or picture one you've seen in a jewelry store. Think about the process it took to design that ring or fashion that gem into a beautiful piece of jewelry. Each time you look at or visualize that ring, breathe a prayer that God will bring something beautiful out of any pain, suffering, or persecution you may experience in the future.

DAILY THOUGHTS & PRAYERS

Day 18

When Loneliness Surrounds You
The One Who Will Never Leave You

*For He Himself has said,
"I will never leave you nor forsake you."*
Hebrews 13:5 NKJV

FROM YOUR FAITHFUL FATHER'S HEART
My child, just like you, all My children have experienced times when they felt surrounded by a black cloud of loneliness and isolation. But on the other side, like the clear sky you see when flying above a cloud in an airplane, you will find the sunlight shining through. I am that light for you, and I am the One who will never leave you. You are never alone because My presence lives inside you and walks with you daily. Do you understand what that means? As My child, no matter how deep the crevice you've descended into, and no matter how far away the light appears, you cannot quench My love or grace. It will always come shining through. When you ask, I will also provide a Christian friend to help you through times of need. But even when you are alone, remember that I have good plans for you, and My mercies are new every morning. I will be with you on every side until the end of your journey. I will never leave you or fail you.

FROM A GRATEFUL HEART
Lord, I've felt the pangs of loneliness as if I were invisible, even in a crowd. I remember times when I cowered into a ball, so lonely for human touch—or Yours, Lord. But You've always been there, waiting for me to call on You. And without fail, Your faithful arms reached around me, drawing me close, whispering to me, "I'm here." Lord, when loneliness threatens my world, and it seems as though no one cares, I choose to depend on You through it all. Thank You that when others turn away, or when I lose the ones I count on, You are still there. You are the One who will never leave me. You are my constant companion and comfort. I choose to believe that You are on the

other side of that cloud, encouraging me, lifting me, and empowering me to hold my head up and keep going. No matter how lonely I feel, by faith I believe Your presence surrounds me, cushioning me on every side, and escorting me to the finish line. With You, I am never alone.

DAILY TRUTH
Alone never means lonely when God is by your side.

DAILY REFLECTIONS
"Do not be afraid or discouraged, for the LORD will personally go ahead of you. He will be with you; he will neither fail you nor abandon you." Deuteronomy 31:8 NLT

"I know what I'm doing. I have it all planned out—plans to take care of you, not abandon you, plans to give you the future you hope for." Jeremiah 29:11 MSG

The faithful love of the LORD never ends! His mercies never cease. Lamentations 3:22 NLT

The path of the righteous is like the morning sun, shining ever brighter till the full light of day. Proverbs 4:18 NIV

DAILY CHALLENGE
Think about the times you've faced loneliness. Describe those situations and the emotions that you experienced. How do these Bible verses comfort and encourage you? What will you do the next time you feel lonely or isolated? Do you have a Christian friend you can call who will encourage you and pray for you? If not, ask God to give you that kind of friend and help you to be one as well.

DAILY THOUGHTS & PRAYERS

Day 19

When You Don't Understand God's Discipline
The One Who Disciplines Those He Loves

> *For the Lord disciplines those He loves,*
> *and He corrects each one He takes as His own.*
> Hebrews 12:6 VOICE

FROM YOUR FAITHFUL FATHER'S HEART
My child, understanding My nature is impossible with your finite mind. At times, you may think I am harsh and uncaring. But I love you too much not to discipline you. I love you despite who you were or who you think you are. I still bless your obedience and trust—in My way and in My time. I am always pursuing passionately, sometimes allowing pressure to nudge you closer to Me. My instruction, training, and discipline are creative because they mold your character to develop Christ-likeness and allow you to share in My holiness. I give parents that same responsibility, but even their best effort at correction is imperfect. My discipline is perfect, loving, and kind, and lasts all your life. I am the One who disciplines those I love.

FROM A GRATEFUL HEART
Lord, I don't understand Your ways, but I'm so thankful that You love me and treat me like Your beloved child. You deserve to be feared and revered because You are holy, perfect, and just. Why would I choose to disobey or turn away from the very One who loves me so much? No one likes to be disciplined. But even though I may not understand Your divine nature, I know that You are the One who disciplines those You love. Without Your correction and training, I don't know where I'd be. I trust that through Your discipline, You are lovingly forming my character so I can reflect You better.

DAILY TRUTH
God is more concerned with who we are and who we are becoming, rather than who we were.

DAILY REFLECTIONS
Lord, you're so kind and tenderhearted and so patient with people who fail you! Your love is like a flooding river overflowing its banks with kindness. You don't look at us only to find our faults, just so that you can hold a grudge against us. You may discipline us for our many sins, but never as much as we really deserve. Nor do you get even with us for what we've done. Psalm 103:8-10 TPT

Fully embrace God's correction as part of your training, for he is doing what any loving father does for his children. For who has ever heard of a child who never had to be corrected? We all should welcome God's discipline as the validation of authentic sonship. For if we have never once endured his correction it only proves we are strangers and not sons. And isn't it true that we respect our earthly fathers even though they corrected and disciplined us? Then we should demonstrate an even greater respect for God, our spiritual Father, as we submit to his life-giving discipline. Our parents corrected us for the short time of our childhood as it seemed good to them. But God corrects us throughout our lives for our own good, giving us an invitation to share his holiness. Hebrews 12:7-10 TPT

For the Father's discipline comes only from his passionate love and pleasure for you. Even when it seems like his correction is harsh, it's still better than any father on earth gives to his child. Proverbs 3:12 TPT

Blessings on all who reverence and trust the Lord—on all who obey him! Psalm 128:1 TLB

DAILY CHALLENGE

Do these verses give you a new perspective on God's discipline? How should parental discipline mirror the way God corrects us? Think about what your life would be like without any loving training or discipline—even by God. Thank Him that He cares enough to help form your character through loving discipline.

DAILY THOUGHTS & PRAYERS

Day 20

When You Feel Broken
The One Who Reshapes Your Life

Yet you, LORD, are our Father.
We are the clay; you are the potter.
We are all the work of your hand.
Isaiah 64:8 NIV

FROM YOUR FAITHFUL FATHER'S HEART
My child, if you could see a potter work at his factory, you'd be amazed at the entire process and what he can fashion from a dull piece of clay. Sometimes he'll smash the entire piece and start over. But when he's finished, the vase he designs belongs in a fine art gallery. Do you sometimes feel like a broken piece of pottery? I will always be working on you, and in you, shaping your life like a lump of clay. What you see as flaws, I see as opportunities to remake you into a useable vessel for My pleasure. My work may seem like a crushing blow from a skillful potter, as I reshape your image and repair the broken pieces. But be patient. I am still the Potter, the One who reshapes your life, and I've designed only the best for you. I want your life to honor Me and to reveal My beauty. I know your weaknesses. The result of My work is not up to you. Whether you feel like a vase sitting on a shelf, a pitcher that's emptied daily, or a cracked pot that leaks, remember that I am not through with you yet. Simply rest in My hands, and let Me do My work. I am the only One who can turn brokenness into usefulness.

FROM A GRATEFUL HEART
Lord, sometimes I've felt like Humpty Dumpty, as if my life had broken into a thousand pieces. Others tried to help, but no one knew how to make me whole again. Then You showed up. You placed me back on Your potter's wheel and carefully, meticulously worked a miracle. Thank You for patiently shaping me with Your loving hands and for helping me to be more like You. Brokenness is a good thing because it's the starting place where

I realize my need for You. Brokenness can empty my pride. I confess my impatience and tendency to circumvent the waiting. There are no instant makeovers. From the chaos of my life, You are always fashioning me into the person You want me to be. You are the faithful One who reshapes my life. I will always be in the process of becoming until You take me home.

DAILY TRUTH
Jesus loves to give spiritual makeovers.

DAILY REFLECTIONS
But this beautiful treasure is contained in us—cracked pots made of earth and clay—so that the transcendent character of this power will be clearly seen as coming from God and not from us. 2 Corinthians 4:7 VOICE

You turn things upside down, as if the potter were thought to be like the clay! Shall what is formed say to the one who formed it, "You did not make me"? Can the pot say to the potter, "You know nothing"? Isaiah 29:16 NIV

But the pot he was shaping from the clay was marred in his hands; so the potter formed it into another pot, shaping it as seemed best to him. Jeremiah 18:4 NIV

I pray with great faith for you, because I'm fully convinced that the One who began this gracious work in you will faithfully continue the process of maturing you until the unveiling of our Lord Jesus Christ! Philippians 1:6 TPT

DAILY CHALLENGE
Read Judges 7, especially verses 15-22. What shone through when the pitchers were broken? Compare that experience with 2 Corinthians 4:7. In what ways have you ever felt broken? How did you handle those situations? If you have never seen a potter working or never bought a piece of pottery, visit a potter at work if you can. Or watch an online video of a potter shaping clay. Thank God that He uses broken vessels for His glory.

DAILY THOUGHTS & PRAYERS

Day 21

When You Need to Hear from God
The One Who Hears and Answers Your Prayers

*I love the Lord because he hears
my prayers and answers them.*
Psalm 116:1 TLB

FROM YOUR FAITHFUL FATHER'S HEART

My child, have I ever failed to meet your needs? Have I ever turned My back on you? My answers are always on time, even when it seems like I'm not listening or can't hear you. I am still the faithful One who hears and answers your prayers. Sometimes you ask for things that will satisfy your wants, not your needs. But My Spirit may reveal that your prayers—and even your heart—need changing. Sometimes My answer is "Not now," and you allow your impatience to grow into anger. The idea of asking and receiving may remain a mystery to you when I already know your needs. I still want you to ask because I love for you to call on Me. I hear the sighs and cries of all My children. Before you even speak a word, I have the answer. Before you even recognize your need, I have the supply. Watch. Wait. Listen. And most of all believe. Ask for things according to My will and in My name with a desire to honor Me. In My perfect timing, the answer you need will become evident to you. Or I will give you peace, even when I say no. I love to give you even more than you can ask or imagine.

FROM A GRATEFUL HEART

Lord, You've told me to ask in Your name. And You've promised to supply my needs. Over and over, Lord, You've done that. But in my impatience, I sometimes look to others for answers instead of asking You. I fixate on my circumstances rather than focus on You and Your promises. And in my foolishness, I take shortcuts that lead me to disaster. Forgive me when I don't trust Your timetable. You always know best. I'll keep knocking, asking, waiting, and believing. You are the One who hears and answers my prayers. Lord, You are amazing.

DAILY TRUTH
God loves to say yes to His children.

DAILY REFLECTIONS
Now to him who is able to do immeasurably more than all we ask or imagine, according to his power that is at work within us, to him be glory in the church and in Christ Jesus throughout all generations, for ever and ever! Amen. Ephesians 3:20-21 NIV

For everyone who keeps on asking receives, and he who keeps on seeking finds, and to him who keeps on knocking, it will be opened. Matthew 7:8 AMP

"This is GOD's Message, the God who made earth, made it livable and lasting, known everywhere as GOD: 'Call to me and I will answer you. I'll tell you marvelous and wondrous things that you could never figure out on your own.'" Jeremiah 33:2-3 MSG

You do not have because you have chosen not to ask. And when you do ask, you still do not get what you want because your motives are all wrong—because you continually focus on self-indulgence. James 4:2-3 VOICE

DAILY CHALLENGE
After studying these verses, jot down three things you are asking God to give you or to do for you. In what way do you think these would honor God? If possible, find a Bible promise that gives you confidence for what you are asking God (by using a keyword such as faith, grace, comfort, etc.). Can you ask and leave the answer to Him?

DAILY THOUGHTS & PRAYERS

Day 22

When You Need Stability
The One Who Never Changes His Mind

"God is not human, that he should lie,
not a human being, that he should change his mind.
Does he speak and then not act?
Does he promise and not fulfill?"
Numbers 23:19 NIV

FROM YOUR FAITHFUL FATHER'S HEART
My child, so much of your worries and fears result in a lack of trust and understanding. I never lie, and My thoughts and actions are not like yours. If I set something in motion, it will continue to the end. I know My purposes for kings, presidents, and rulers of nations. No one can change My nature. I drew a line between good and evil from the beginning. My creation chose foolishly and suffered the consequences. But I also formed a plan for the world's salvation. I promise eternity to those who receive My forgiveness and love. I will never act any differently than who I am. Holiness, justice, righteousness, goodness, faithfulness—these all describe Me well. And they always will. I am not faithful one day, and uncaring the next. I don't promise something and then fail to deliver. I am still the One who never changes His mind. You may fail to keep your word and even forget what you've promised. But My words last forever. You will always need My stability. And I'm waiting to give it to you.

FROM A GRATEFUL HEART
Lord, sometimes I say one thing, and then do another. I make promises I can never fulfill and break the ones I can. I want to do the right thing, but my human nature interferes. I am the one who needs not only my mind to be changed, but my whole body, mind, and spirit to be conformed to You. Others depend on me. And I want to reestablish my complete dependency on You. Lord, You are the One who never changes Your mind. That means

You are faithful and dependable at all times. With Your stability, I can keep moving forward.

DAILY TRUTH
The only thing that ever needs changing about our relationship with God is us.

DAILY REFLECTIONS
"You know with all your heart and soul that not one of all the good promises the Lord your God gave you has failed. Every promise has been fulfilled; not one has failed." Joshua 23:14 NIV

He will be your constant source of stability in changing times, and out of his abundant love he gives you the riches of salvation, wisdom, and knowledge. Yes, the fear of the Lord is the key to this treasure! Isaiah 33:6 TPT

For God did not send his Son into the world to condemn the world, but to save the world through him. John 3:17 NIV

Let everyone be subject to the governing authorities, for there is no authority except that which God has established. The authorities that exist have been established by God. Romans 13:1 NIV

DAILY CHALLENGE
Ask the Lord to remind you of any promises you have made to Him or others but failed to keep. If there are any you can still fulfill, ask for His help in accomplishing that. If you have broken any promises to others, seek their forgiveness, and confess it to your faithful Father. Write down any other names God lays on your heart and when you will talk to them.

DAILY THOUGHTS & PRAYERS

Day 23

When You Need a Hero
The One Who Is Mighty to Save

"It is I, the Lord, announcing your salvation;
I, the Lord, the one who is mighty to save!"
Isaiah 63:1 TLB

FROM YOUR FAITHFUL FATHER'S HEART

My child, remember the stories where battles between good and evil held you spellbound? Tales where you waited breathlessly, longing for the hero to appear at just the right moment and rescue you? In real life, your foolish efforts to find that hero may lead you to dangerous paths of self-destruction. At times you may have blamed others for the wrong in My world. And you may have even looked in the wrong places and followed deceitful leaders hoping to find solutions. But when you need a hero, I am still the only One who is mighty to save. I am the only One who can bring salvation to the world. I've designed My plan with love and sealed it with My blood. My Word is not the diary of a wimpy God, but the powerful, living story of love to all people. I didn't come to rescue you with weapons of warfare. I could have saved Myself, but I offered My life voluntarily in payment for your sins. I didn't come to save the day; I came to save the world. Others may try to persuade you with strange philosophies and fleshly rules, but I became the perfect, flawless sacrifice for you—your true hero. And one day, when I return for My children, all will celebrate Me as the true hero and Savior of the world.

FROM A GRATEFUL HEART

Lord, I love to read fictional stories of true heroes. But they can't help me in my earthly fight for survival. I'm tired of fighting my battles alone. I'm not strong enough without Your help. I confess there have been times when I've looked to others instead of You for my rescue. With one breath You could have destroyed me. Yet You chose to give me salvation. Not only that,

You fight for me daily. C. S. Lewis pictured You metaphorically as the Lion Aslan in his book, *Narnia*. You are the great Lion of Judah, the One who is mighty to save, and the One who can trample down my enemies. What a mighty God and Savior You are! Thank You for rescuing me. You'll always be my hero.

DAILY TRUTH
In real life, Jesus is the only Hero we need.

DAILY REFLECTIONS
"No one else can save us. Indeed, we can be saved only by the power of the one named Jesus and not by any other person." Acts 4:12 GW

He came once for all, at the end of the age, to put away the power of sin forever by dying for us. Hebrews 9:26 TLB

For you stand beside me as my hero who rescues me. I've seen with my own eyes the defeat of my enemies. I've triumphed over them all! Psalm 118:7 TPT

"Praise be to the exalted Lord God of Israel, for he has seen us through eyes of grace, and he comes as our Hero-God to set us free!" Luke 1:68 TPT

DAILY CHALLENGE
List your favorite hero characters from childhood, or think about the ones you've read in books or seen in movies. Describe their limitations. Who are your heroes in the Bible? Write down as many as you can name. How do all of them compare to Jesus as your all-time Hero?

DAILY THOUGHTS & PRAYERS

Day 24

When You Don't Know What to Pray
The One Who Intercedes for You

*In the same way, the Spirit helps us in our weakness.
We do not know what we ought to pray for,
but the Spirit himself intercedes for us through wordless groans.
And he who searches our hearts knows the mind of the Spirit,
because the Spirit intercedes for God's people
in accordance with the will of God.*
Romans 8:26-27 NIV

FROM YOUR FAITHFUL FATHER'S HEART
My child, you'll experience so many times when you come into My presence without the faintest idea how to express yourself. How could I, the Holy One, hear your prayers in the first place? At times, you even feel like a child whose vocabulary hasn't progressed beyond kindergarten. Don't worry about knowing the right words to say when you talk to Me. I hear your heart. When you need an intercessor, My Spirit searches your heart and sees the deepest desires hidden there. You will also have moments when your pain is so deep you cannot even speak. Tears cloud your heart, and words refuse to come. Whether you feel helpless, lonely, broken, or sad, I know your need. And when you don't know how or what to pray for others? You're not alone. Because My ways are different from yours, you won't always understand what to pray. Don't let that stop you from pouring out your heart to Me, either in tearful cries or spoken words. My Spirit will take those groanings and form them into a prayer that is My will for you. In time, I will give you peace about those issues. When you don't know what to say, I am still the One who intercedes for you—perfectly.

FROM A GRATEFUL HEART
Lord, sometimes I feel tongue-tied when I step onto holy ground. What can I say to the One who left heaven for me? How can I communicate

with the God who created all things, the One who holds the world in His hands? Other times, the hurts in my heart are like boulders so great that I can't possibly move them. Words hide in the broken places of my soul. Thank You for reminding me that You hear the deepest needs of my heart, even when I can't verbalize them. Thank You that You are the One who intercedes for me as I pray for others, and You also offer intercession against the power of sin in my own life. You know me so well. Purify the desires of my heart, Lord, so that the motives behind my requests are not solely to relieve my pain or discomfort, but to glorify You in the situation, no matter what happens.

DAILY TRUTH
When God hears you pray, He focuses on your heart, not your words.

DAILY REFLECTIONS
In her deep anguish Hannah prayed to the LORD, weeping bitterly. 1 Samuel 1:10 NIV

Therefore he is able, once and forever, to save those who come to God through him. He lives forever to intercede with God on their behalf. Hebrews 7:25 NLT

From the ends of the earth, I cry to you for help when my heart is overwhelmed. Psalm 61:2 NLT

I am exhausted and completely crushed. My groans come from an anguished heart. Psalm 38:8 NLT

DAILY CHALLENGE

Do you have difficulty praying? Does your mind start wandering toward yesterday's events or tomorrow's worries each time you close your eyes? Does the pain in your heart seem too heavy to share? Today, spend several minutes in silence, then a few moments writing, giving thanks for things God has done, and offering praise to Him using descriptive words about His character (holy, loving, compassionate, patient, etc.). Then instead of trying to form words into a prayer petition, simply speak or write one-word "breath" prayers that describe the needs of your heart right now (Help! Wisdom! Strength!) Ask the Holy Spirit to form even your unspoken groans into a prayer that will honor Him.

DAILY THOUGHTS & PRAYERS

Day 25

When You Need a Patient Father
The One Who Is Slow to Get Angry

The Lord is slow to get angry; but his power is great.
Nahum 1:3 NLT

FROM YOUR FAITHFUL FATHER'S HEART
My child, why do you sometimes wonder if I am angry with you? You can't gauge My character by your circumstances or your raw emotions. My patience never runs out, and My nature is unchangeable. Those who oppose Me will experience My discipline and the consequences of their choices, yet I desire to condemn no one. Some even mistake My consuming, jealous fire of love for them as destructive anger. As a holy God, I cannot tolerate sin, but I created a loving plan from the very beginning of time. If you know Me intimately, you will experience both My patient grace and great power. Even though I could destroy everything I've made in a heartbeat, I am still the One who is slow to get angry. I've chosen to allow you to turn to Me and live in a close relationship forever. It's not My lack of patience that prevents you from experiencing the fullness of life. My spiritual laws are still at work. But Jesus' death satisfied My holy, righteous anger. I will draw you to Myself, again and again, gently working with you. I am still a faithful, patient Father, always caring, nurturing, and guiding you with grace and wisdom.

FROM A GRATEFUL HEART
Lord, I'm so grateful You are a patient Father who treats Your children not with anger, but with love. In my selfishness and warped thinking, I've misunderstood Your character, Your power, and even Your intentions. Why have you been so patient with me? Despite how undeserving I am, You still wrap me in Your tender and forgiving arms. Help me to love others the way You love me. Forgive me for my foolish tantrums and wrong conclusions. I long to exchange anger for gentleness. Thank You for being the One who is

slow to get angry. Thank You, Lord, for Your incredible patience.

DAILY TRUTH
Releasing the power of God's love keeps us from unleashing the anger inside our hearts.

DAILY REFLECTIONS
For God did not send his Son into the world to condemn the world, but to save the world through him. Whoever believes in him is not condemned, but whoever does not believe stands condemned already because they have not believed in the name of God's one and only Son. John 3:17-18 NIV

The Lord isn't really being slow about his promise, as some people think. No, he is being patient for your sake. He does not want anyone to be destroyed, but wants everyone to repent. 2 Peter 3:9 NLT

"For the Lord your God is a consuming fire; He is a jealous (impassioned) God [demanding what is rightfully and uniquely His]." Deuteronomy 4:24 AMP

The Lord then passed in front of him and called out, "I, the Lord, am a God who is full of compassion and pity, who is not easily angered and who shows great love and faithfulness." Exodus 34:6 GNT

DAILY CHALLENGE
In Exodus 33, Moses asked to see God's glory. So God agreed to allow Moses to see the afterglow of His glory as He passed by. What do you think about the way God described Himself to Moses in Exodus 34:6? How would you describe Him?

DAILY THOUGHTS & PRAYERS

Day 26

When the Present Seems Like an Eternity
The One Who Inhabits Eternity

*The high and lofty One who inhabits eternity,
the Holy One, says this:
I live in that high and holy place
where those with contrite, humble spirits dwell;
and I refresh the humble and give new courage
to those with repentant hearts.*
Isaiah 57:15 TLB

FROM YOUR FAITHFUL FATHER'S HEART
My child, you've often questioned, "How long will this last?" Life freezes and locks you into an endless, repetitive cycle. You may feel like a hamster running in circles on an eternal treadmill or a trapped rat glued to one spot, unable to retreat or advance. But I will show you that eternity is not a hopeless cycle, but a hopeful promise. It's not an unwelcome status, but a joyful gift. Eternity is My home, and yet I live in your heart, too. And forever with Me is such a contrast to your earthly struggles. For you, eternity begins the moment you say "Yes" to Me. Life then becomes not only bearable but victorious. Yes, you'll still face problems on earth, but I will turn your ruts into roads—an eternal pathway forever with Me. I am still the One who inhabits eternity. Even though you may never understand that, I have bridged the gap between death and life. Your situation won't last forever, but I will. I will lift up and restore all who choose humility over pride.

FROM A GRATEFUL HEART
Lord, I can't even begin to fathom eternity. That sounds so long and far away. Some days all I can think about is survival—getting through another day. Defeat hangs around like a dark thundercloud, threatening to shut me down. Whether I struggle with old habits or unchanging circumstances in my world, I often entertain thoughts like, "Why try, anyway?" But to-

day, Lord, I humble myself before You. You are high and holy, beyond any earthly definition; yet You chose to heal my selfish, rebellious heart, and make me Your own. Both now, and forever, Lord, You are the One who inhabits eternity. And that's where I choose to stay.

DAILY TRUTH
Eternity is our true, forever home.

DAILY REFLECTIONS
"Very truly I tell you, whoever hears my word and believes him who sent me has eternal life and will not be judged but has crossed over from death to life." John 5:24 NIV

Death once held us in its grip, and by the blunder of one man, death reigned as king over humanity. But now, how much more are we held in the grip of grace and continue reigning as kings in life, enjoying our regal freedom through the gift of perfect righteousness in the one and only Jesus, the Messiah! Romans 5:17 TPT

But thank God! He gives us victory over sin and death through our Lord Jesus Christ. 1 Corinthians 15:57 NLT

Humble yourselves before the Lord, and he will lift you up. James 4:10 NIV

DAILY CHALLENGE
Place a metal or plastic ring near your workspace or where you will see it often. Picture that ring as a choice you can make: (1) Live your life running in needless circles that travel nowhere or (2) See life as an eternal, never-ending circle of joy that begins and ends with Jesus.

DAILY THOUGHTS & PRAYERS

Day 27

When the Future Seems Uncertain
The One Who Holds Tomorrow

*Good people pass away; the godly often die before their time.
But no one seems to care or wonder why.
No one seems to understand
that God is protecting them from the evil to come.*
Isaiah 57:1 NLT

FROM YOUR FAITHFUL FATHER'S HEART
My child, I know when your heart aches at the loss of a loved one, a friend, or someone whose life is making such a difference in this world. Their death seems premature and unfair. You often misunderstand the suffering of those who stand for Me around the world. When sin entered My world, the tension between good and evil stretched tighter. The pure evil nature of others confuses you, especially when believers don't escape their hands. You can't see the future, but I know what's coming. I deal with nations, kings, and presidents. I am still the One who holds tomorrow, the One who protects you from coming evil—the kind of godlessness you can't even imagine. I see the bigger picture, and I am always thinking of My children. Your knowledge is incomplete. If you make this world your home, fear and discouragement will set in. I am the One who determines when your work here is finished. I know the evil intent of man's heart, and that death is also a merciful deliverance from even worse things to come.

FROM A GRATEFUL HEART
Lord, at times I feel like a rubber band, pulled between going home to You, and staying here in a sinful world. Fear and frustration rise to the surface. What will the future bring? What will my children and grandchildren experience? I don't always understand Your promise of protection. Does it include physical, temporary safety, or eternal, spiritual security? And how can I make a difference in the presence of such unwanted atrocities? Some-

times it seems there is so little I can do, especially when life is such a puzzle. You are the only One who knows what will happen in the days to come. But my hope is in this: Your wisdom, protection, and love are more powerful than the evil forces on earth. And because I belong to You, I will not fear the future. Your goodness and mercy pursue me daily. I am safe, trusting You in all things, whether they appear to be good or not. Thank You for Your protection. Thank You that You are the One who holds tomorrow and the future in Your hands.

DAILY TRUTH
Security is being safely held in Jesus' hands.

DAILY REFLECTIONS
So why would I fear the future? Only goodness and tender love pursue me all the days of my life. Then afterward, when my life is through, I'll return to your glorious presence to be forever with you! Psalm 23:6 TPT

Trust in him at all times, you people; pour out your hearts to him, for God is our refuge. Psalm 62:8 NIV

Now we see things imperfectly, like puzzling reflections in a mirror, but then we will see everything with perfect clarity. All that I know now is partial and incomplete, but then I will know everything completely, just as God now knows me completely. 1 Corinthians 13:12 NLT

Friends, this world is not your home, so don't make yourselves cozy in it. 1 Peter 2:11 MSG

DAILY CHALLENGE
What causes you to feel uncertain about the future? List your reasons. How difficult is it for you to trust your future to God? Does it help to remember that your home on earth is only temporary? What other truths about God's faithfulness give you security for the future?

DAILY THOUGHTS & PRAYERS

Day 28

When You Need a Friend
The One Who Makes You His Friend

*So now we can rejoice
in our wonderful new relationship with God
because our Lord Jesus Christ has made us friends of God.*
Romans 5:11 NLT

FROM YOUR FAITHFUL FATHER'S HEART
My child, I am not your enemy. I never was. But sin stole from you and all those I created for My glory. Sin became the enemy and the barrier between us. That's why My Son died for you. He played the part of the enemy, by taking all your sin upon Himself, giving you freedom. You belong to Me now, because you have chosen to receive His death and freedom for yourself. I am the One who makes you My friend. I demolished the chasm between My holiness and your sinfulness. Now there is a way to approach Me. I want to share with you, as an intimate friend, and I want you to know My heart. Keep our friendship strong by fellowshipping and communicating with Me daily. Should sin find a crevice in your heart, come to Me and admit it immediately. My forgiveness is yours, and I will restore that broken fellowship. I am a holy God, but I still call you My friend. I treasure our friendship, My child! Don't let anything try to come between us.

FROM A GRATEFUL HEART
Lord, to be a friend of God sounds so impossible. Abraham? Yes. Moses? Absolutely. Great men and women of God in the Bible? Of course! But who am I that You would value me enough to call me Your friend? I am so grateful that You didn't require me to follow a set of rules for Your approval. You didn't wait to see if I would clean up my act before You chose me as Your friend. Instead, through Jesus' death and resurrection, You made friendship possible. No friendship in this world compares to Yours, Lord. Thank You for bridging the gap so I could know You and love You. I want

our relationship to grow sweeter every day.

DAILY TRUTH
Friendship with God is by reservation only—but is available to all who choose Him as Lord.

DAILY REFLECTIONS
But if we freely admit our sins when his light uncovers them, he will be faithful to forgive us every time. God is just to forgive us our sins because of Christ, and he will continue to cleanse us from all unrighteousness. 1 John 1:9 TPT

For Christ has entered into heaven itself to appear now before God as our Friend. Hebrews 9:24 TLB

But now you belong to Christ Jesus, and though you once were far away from God, now you have been brought very near to him because of what Jesus Christ has done for you with his blood. Ephesians 2:13 TLB

For he has dedicated a new, life-giving way for us to approach God. For just as the veil was torn in two, Jesus' body was torn open to give us free and fresh access to him! Hebrews 10:20 TPT

DAILY CHALLENGE
What do you talk about with friends? How are your earthly friendships different than your friendship with God? How would your prayer life change if you talked to God as if He were your best friend? What would you like to ask Him? What would you like to tell Him? Write a prayer to God with the assurance that He is your best friend.

DAILY THOUGHTS & PRAYERS

Day 29

When God's Creation Amazes You
The One Who Stretches Out the Heavens

The L<small>ORD</small> wraps himself in light as with a garment;
he stretches out the heavens like a tent.
Psalm 104:2 NIV

FROM YOUR FAITHFUL FATHER'S HEART
My child, how do you describe My holiness or majestic handiwork? You can't ascribe finite words to My infinite being or My creation. I am the One who stretches out the heavens like a tent over the earth. I am clothed in light and dazzling purity, so bright you can't gaze into My face and live. Yet I am the same One who created such a stunning world and the same God who first formed man from the dust. Day after day, you awake to the color of My creativity: from purple, majestic mountains, to the brilliance of red, gold, and blue flowers, to the incredible variety of birds and animals. Clouds ride like chariots across the skies, all at My command. I placed you and all My creation under that heavenly canopy to live on earth. Yet I am also the faithful God you can call your Father.

FROM A GRATEFUL HEART
Father, You are indeed a wonder, and Your world is wonder-full. When I stand in the presence of Your beautiful creation, I long for words to describe its magnitude. Sometimes, all I can utter is, "Hallelujah!" with arms reached toward heaven. Other times, only tears of gratitude will testify to Your magnificence. Nothing is so healing to my soul as being in Your vast creation, seeing how huge and majestic You are, how small I am, and yet realizing that You love me. As the One who stretches out the heavens, Your purity and brightness radiate through the clouds, blinding us with Your greatness. How awesome that You not only created a shelter to cover us on earth; You also paved a road to the heavens, accessible through Christ's death and resurrection. My eyes can't see, and my heart can barely grasp

the miracle You provided. But by faith, I visualize the home beyond that heavenly canopy that will be mine one day—the place I will dwell forever with You.

DAILY TRUTH
The greatness of God is beyond description, but not beyond belief.

DAILY REFLECTIONS
Yahweh, our Lord, how magnificent is Your name throughout the earth! You have covered the heavens with Your majesty. Psalm 8:1 HCSB

"But," he said, "you cannot see my face, for no one may see me and live." Exodus 33:20 NIV

And the LORD God formed man of the dust of the ground, and breathed into his nostrils the breath of life; and man became a living soul. Genesis 2:7 KJV

This Good News tells us that God makes us ready for heaven—makes us right in God's sight—when we put our faith and trust in Christ to save us. Romans 1:17 TLB

DAILY CHALLENGE
Spend a few moments meditating on Psalm 8. On a clear day, step outside your home, office, or wherever you are and observe the heavens and God's creation. Or imagine a beautiful place you have visited. What words would you use to express the magnificence of God and His creation? Write your own psalm or prayer of praise to God for His wonderful handiwork.

DAILY THOUGHTS & PRAYERS

Day 30

When You Want to Flip Your Failures
The One Who Calls You Forward

Brothers and sisters, I do not consider that I have made it my own yet; but one thing I do: forgetting what lies behind and reaching forward to what lies ahead, I press on toward the goal to win the [heavenly] prize of the upward call of God in Christ Jesus.
Philippians 3:13-14 AMP

FROM YOUR FAITHFUL FATHER'S HEART
My child, why does the fear of failure cripple you? Even as My follower, you may fall at times. But that doesn't mean failure. I am the One who calls you forward, not backward. I already know your shortcomings and weaknesses. I see your heart, and I've already forgiven you. But your confession keeps our fellowship sweet. As long as I give you breath to live for Me, I will keep calling you to press on toward the goal and the "well done" that waits for you. I don't base success on your accomplishments, but on your relationship with Me. Learn from your mistakes, as well as your victories. Lay them all at My feet. And when you honor Me, I will give you the kind of success I want for you. I will help you achieve the dreams I designed for you if you will delight yourself in Me and let My Spirit fill you with God-confidence.

FROM A GRATEFUL HEART
Lord, I'm so hard on myself at times. All I see is one failure after another, and that makes me anxious about the future. Will I ever feel successful at anything? But then You remind me that success is not at all what I thought. You're interested more in my character, not my accomplishments. You are strengthening me constantly for the journey You've designed for me, and You enjoy my fellowship. Flip the failures of my past, Lord. Let them become steppingstones to future dreams, as I allow You to teach me what I did wrong, or where I failed to keep my eyes on You. Today, I'm releasing

my past failures and successes. You can have them all. What I want is to know You more, Lord. To honor You and love You more deeply—that's my desire. You are the One who calls me forward, and with Your help, that's the direction I want to go.

DAILY TRUTH
Falling does not always equal failing.

DAILY REFLECTIONS
Do not grieve over your past mistakes. Let the Eternal's own joy be your protection! Nehemiah 8:10 VOICE

For the lovers of God may suffer adversity and stumble seven times, but they will continue to rise over and over again. Proverbs 24:16 TPT

Therefore let us [with privilege] approach the throne of grace [that is, the throne of God's gracious favor] with confidence and without fear, so that we may receive mercy [for our failures] and find [His amazing] grace to help in time of need [an appropriate blessing, coming just at the right moment]. Hebrews 4:16 AMP

Take delight in the Lord, and he will give you the desires of your heart. Psalm 37:4 NIV

DAILY CHALLENGE
Are you holding on to any failures from the past? What successes have you experienced? Write down your definition of success and failure. How do these verses encourage you? Memorize Philippians 3:13-14 in your favorite translation or paraphrase. Review it every day for a week until you can remember it wherever you go.

DAILY THOUGHTS & PRAYERS

Day 31

When All You See Is Darkness
The One Who Lights Your Darkness

You light a lamp for me. The Lord, *my God, lights up my darkness.*
Psalm 18:28 NLT

FROM YOUR FAITHFUL FATHER'S HEART
My child, you will experience dark days when you long for a corner of sunshine to slip through the cracks. Your enemy may attempt to cloud your mind and depress your spirits. Many will hate you and criticize you during your life, just because you belong to Me. But the time will come when I will exchange your groaning for My glory. Darkness will never cast its shadow on your heart again. I am still the Lord your God, the Everlasting Light, the One who lights your darkness. As the Light of the World, I have already brought an unquenchable flame to the hearts of those who will receive Me. But I will not shine the full light of My glory until a time known only to Me. When My calendar has flipped the final page, there will be no need for sun or moon. I will be your light forever. Until then, cling to the hope I have given you, and follow My light that brightens your path, one day at a time. I have the power to make your darkness flee.

FROM A GRATEFUL HEART
Lord, some days I can barely see beyond this hour or this minute. My enemy will use fear, exhaustion, or stress to send me into a temporary, emotional tailspin. Yet I cling to the truth that in Jesus' name, You will bring light and hope to my dark tunnel. You will provide the help I need. I long for the time when all darkness will cease, and when all will acknowledge You for who You are. Thank You for the times I stumbled in the dark, only to realize You were constantly holding my hand and guiding my feet. You truly are the One who lights my darkness. You are my Everlasting Light. The spark You ignited in my heart years ago has grown into a full-blown flame. My yearning to know You completely grows stronger and brighter.

One day all darkness will cease. How I look forward to that day, Lord!

DAILY TRUTH
The smallest candle flame is better than no light at all.

DAILY REFLECTIONS
"No longer will you need the sun to shine by day, nor the moon to give its light by night, for the LORD your God will be your everlasting light, and your God will be your glory." Isaiah 60:19 NLT

"If the world hates you, keep in mind that it hated me first." John 15:18 NIV

"I am the Light of the world. So if you follow me, you won't be stumbling through the darkness, for living light will flood your path." John 8:12 TLB

And there will be no night there—no need for lamps or sun—for the Lord God will be their light; and they shall reign forever and ever. Revelation 22:5 TLB

DAILY CHALLENGE
Have you ever experienced "dark" times in your life? Describe them. How long did they last? As you reflect on those experiences, what do you think caused them? How did God bring you through them? What keeps people from seeing Jesus as the Light of the World? Have you ever felt persecution because you were a child of God? How can you be a light to others who are still living in darkness? Thank God that He is your light in the darkness and that His light is enough for your needs.

DAILY THOUGHTS & PRAYERS

Day 32

When Your Life Feels Empty
The One Who Is Your Salvation and Joy

Yet I will rejoice in the Lord!
I will be joyful in the God of my salvation!
Habakkuk 3:18 NLT

FROM YOUR FAITHFUL FATHER'S HEART
My child, you experience times of drought when your life appears empty and barren. You work hard, yet the results show nothing for your labor. Friendships may falter; efforts may fail. The things you hold dear slip through your fingers like sand. Months may pass and you feel caught in a time warp that never ends. In those times, remember that I am still your faithful Father, the One who is your salvation and joy. I ransomed you for a high price. What I began in you, I will finish, even though you see no improvement. Are you willing to exercise a *no-matter-what* faith? Trust Me daily for the things you can't see, feel, hear, or produce. I want you to focus on Me and our relationship. Let your *I can* turn into *I will*. When you decide that no matter what happens, you will set your heart on Me, I will take care of the emptiness and fill you with My joy.

FROM A GRATEFUL HEART
Lord, sometimes I hear myself crying out to You like a child. The joy has drained from my heart, and I see the nakedness of my existence. I try to face each day with courage and confidence, but when I see nothing on the horizon to encourage me, my praise turns to empty words. I need something or someone to tell me it will be okay, that "this, too shall pass." But in my weakness, You step in and remind me of my beginnings. Just like when I was young, I run to You, Lord. You were; You are; You will be God: the One who is my salvation and joy. And though outward circumstances may not change, I will, Lord. I choose to find my joy in You, no matter what happens around me.

DAILY TRUTH
Because joy is our choice, we can always rejoice.

DAILY REFLECTIONS
"But blessed are those who trust in the Lord and have made the Lord their hope and confidence. They are like trees planted along a riverbank, with roots that reach deep into the water. Such trees are not bothered by the heat or worried by long months of drought. Their leaves stay green, and they never stop producing fruit." Jeremiah 17:7-8 NLT

For you know that your lives were ransomed once and for all from the empty and futile way of life handed down from generation to generation. It was not a ransom payment of silver and gold, which eventually perishes, but the precious blood of Christ—who like a spotless, unblemished lamb was sacrificed for us. 1 Peter 1:18-19 TPT

And I am certain that God, who began the good work within you, will continue his work until it is finally finished on the day when Christ Jesus returns. Philippians 1:6 NLT

For salvation comes from God. What joys he gives to all his people. Psalm 3:8 TLB

DAILY CHALLENGE
Read Habakkuk 3:17-19. How does the prophet Habakkuk respond to troubled times? Write down the things that can drain you at times. As you pray today, hold an empty glass in your hand, representing your emptiness apart from the Lord. Then fill that glass with water. Ask the Lord to fill you with joy again, no matter what comes your way.

DAILY THOUGHTS & PRAYERS

Day 33

When Life Doesn't Seem Fair
The One Who Is Perfect and Just

*He is the Rock, his works are perfect, and all his ways are just.
A faithful God who does no wrong, upright and just is he.*
Deuteronomy 32:4 NIV

FROM YOUR FAITHFUL FATHER'S HEART
My child, do you struggle with what is fair? Does your heart cry out for unbiased treatment? You don't see the beginning or the ending of all things, but I do. I know the right action to take at all times. Others seek retaliation for unfair treatment, but you must see things differently. Learn to trust My sense of fairness, not your own. I know when discipline is needed, and I know when mercy will be wise. I am the One who is perfect and just. My works are perfect, but My children don't always act perfectly. If I gave them what they truly deserve, I would be just. But through My death and resurrection, I offer forgiveness to all. I will take care of those who mistreat you. I love them too. I will never act unfairly toward you or any of My creations. Trust Me. I will be more than faithful to you.

FROM A GRATEFUL HEART
Lord, how many times my heart has cried, "Unfair," when I've seen Your children suffer unjustly. And, yes, sometimes I feel that way about myself. Yet there is nothing I could ever do to earn Your favor. I deserve nothing. And judgment belongs to You, not me. Why should I give in to anger? If You could voluntarily experience such a cruel, unjust death, why should I complain about my issues? You truly are a faithful God who does no wrong. You are the One who is perfect and just. Forgive me when I try to take things into my own hands. Thank You for showing mercy to me when I deserved only punishment. I confess my skewed perspective and limited trust. Help me to see Your ways more clearly, Lord.

DAILY TRUTH
If God gave us what we truly deserve, no one could stand before Him.

DAILY REFLECTIONS
It is beautiful how God has done everything at the right time. He has put a sense of eternity in people's minds. Yet, mortals still can't grasp what God is doing from the beginning to the end of time. Ecclesiastes 3:11 GW

*He will rule with fairness and justice from the throne of his ancestor David for all eternity. The passionate commitment of the L*ORD *of Heaven's Armies will make this happen! Isaiah 9:7 NLT*

He does not punish us for all our sins; he does not deal harshly with us, as we deserve. Psalm 103:10 NLT

But you, O Lord, are a God of compassion and mercy, slow to get angry and filled with unfailing love and faithfulness. Psalm 86:15 NLT

DAILY CHALLENGE
In what kind of situations are you tempted to think life is not fair? What about in others' lives? Are there any areas of your life where you are struggling with forgiveness? Have you ever been tempted with thoughts of revenge? In what ways do you feel God has treated you fairly? Read Luke 23:34. How did Jesus deal with those who mistreated Him when He was dying on a cross? Thank God today that He does not give you what you deserve.

DAILY THOUGHTS & PRAYERS

Day 34

When Your Heart Needs Peace
The One Who Gives True Peace

*"I leave the gift of peace with you—my peace.
Not the kind of fragile peace given by the world,
but my perfect peace. Don't yield to fear or be troubled
in your hearts—instead, be courageous!"*
John 14:27 TPT

FROM YOUR FAITHFUL FATHER'S HEART
My child, why do you fret and worry so much? Your heart will experience sorrow, sadness, and confusion at times, just as My disciples did when I left their world and ascended to heaven. But I did not leave them alone, and I will never abandon you either. My Holy Spirit indwells each believer, giving them a comforting peace that cannot be explained by human hearts or minds. If I had never died; if I had never risen from the grave; and if My Holy Spirit—your Counselor and Comforter—had never come, you could never have truly known Me. And you would never have experienced My peace. The world may offer you a temporary, fragile peace, but the gift of peace I offer lasts for eternity. Instead of worrying, tell Me your needs often, and give thanks for My answers. Even if your circumstances don't change, your spirit can still experience a deep-down serenity if you continue to trust Me. I am not only the One who gives true peace; I am your Peace.

FROM A GRATEFUL HEART
Lord, I admit the frailty of my own emotions. Trusting them instead of You sends me into a spiral of negative thinking and isolation. Like a child clinging to her daddy, I would have joined Your disciples and cried out, "Don't leave, Jesus! Don't leave me!" But peace is not a feeling; it is a gift You give to all Your children. How foolish I feel worrying about things that don't matter. So many times I've searched for peace in the chaos of my

circumstances, only to hear Your Spirit silence me with a gentle, "Peace, be still." Thank You, Lord. You—and only You—are the One who gives true, lasting peace.

DAILY TRUTH
We find peace not by looking in, but by looking up.

DAILY REFLECTIONS
You will keep in perfect peace all who trust in you, all whose thoughts are fixed on you! Isaiah 26:3 NLT

Don't worry about anything; instead, pray about everything; tell God your needs, and don't forget to thank him for his answers. If you do this, you will experience God's peace, which is far more wonderful than the human mind can understand. His peace will keep your thoughts and your hearts quiet and at rest as you trust in Christ Jesus. Philippians 4:6-7 TLB

Our reconciling "Peace" is Jesus! Ephesians 2:14 TPT

"But the Counselor, the Holy Spirit—the Father will send Him in My name—will teach you all things and remind you of everything I have told you." John 14:26 HCSB

DAILY CHALLENGE
Write down three things that try to steal your peace. How do you usually react when that happens? How would you like to respond next time? How has Jesus been your Peace? Now write JESUS across that list of things that threaten your peace and cause you to worry. Thank Jesus that He is your Peace and that He gives you peace beyond understanding.

DAILY THOUGHTS & PRAYERS

Day 35

When You Can't Find God
The One Who Can Always Be Found

"Starting from scratch, he made the entire human race and made the earth hospitable, with plenty of time and space for living so we could seek after God, and not just grope around in the dark but actually find him. He doesn't play hide-and-seek with us. He's not remote; he's near. We live and move in him, can't get away from him!"
Acts 17:26-28 MSG

FROM YOUR FAITHFUL FATHER'S HEART
My child, where have you been looking for Me? Do you think I can't hear or see you? I don't play hide-and-seek. If it seems I am hidden, and you cannot find Me, perhaps you are the one hiding. You will still find Me speaking to you through the pages in My Word if you stop long enough to read and listen. I may allow testing to refine you, to help you walk by faith. But even then I have not moved. I am the One who can always be found. My full glory will always be hidden from My creation while you are on earth. But when you pursue Me, you will also experience new joys of discovery, when My presence overtakes you in powerful ways. When you search for Me diligently with all your heart, soul, and mind, you will find Me where I will always be: waiting for you.

FROM A GRATEFUL HEART
Lord, I've felt the lonely desperation of moving away from Your presence, hiding from You, and seeking after things that never satisfy. In those moments, what was I thinking? But what joy I experienced when I searched and found You again. Your Spirit pursued me, sometimes even chasing me until I was safe in Your arms. You are still my faithful Father, the One who can always be found. Thank You for Your patience with me and Your complete forgiveness. You are everything my heart could want. Even when I can't see You, touch You, or feel Your presence around me, I know You are

there, waiting. Lord, I will search for You daily with my whole heart. The thought of discovering Your awesome presence each day fills me with both fearful anticipation and desperate longing. And Your faithful Word says when I seek You, I will always find You.

DAILY TRUTH
God always knows what it takes to bring us back to Him.

DAILY REFLECTIONS
Here's the one thing I crave from God, the one thing I seek above all else: I want the privilege of living with him every moment in his house, finding the sweet loveliness of his face, filled with awe, delighting in his glory and grace. I want to live my life so close to him that he takes pleasure in my every prayer. Psalm 27:4 TPT

"Keep on asking, and you will receive what you ask for. Keep on seeking, and you will find. Keep on knocking, and the door will be opened to you. For everyone who asks, receives. Everyone who seeks, finds. And to everyone who knocks, the door will be opened." Matthew 7:7-8 NLT

So keep on believing what you have been taught from the beginning. If you do, you will always be in close fellowship with both God the Father and his Son. 1 John 2:24 TLB

For you know that when your faith is tested, your endurance has a chance to grow. James 1:3 NLT

DAILY CHALLENGE

Think about the times you played hide-and-seek as a child. Did a friend or sibling ever hide in a place where you couldn't find him? How did you feel? Frustrated? Anxious? Worried? Have you ever tried to hide from God? Aren't you glad you know the One who can always be found? What steps will you take to pursue God more?

DAILY THOUGHTS & PRAYERS

Day 36

When Your Vision Is Limited
The One Who Opens Blind Eyes

The LORD opens the eyes of the blind.
Psalm 146:8 NLT

FROM YOUR FAITHFUL FATHER'S HEART
My child, those who read braille are not the only ones without sight. Some are also spiritually blind. You know what that's like. You walked into a situation unprepared, and unexpected circumstances blindsided you. Perhaps bouts of false guilt or depression severed your sight temporarily. Remember what your life was like before you met Me? Most of My children identify with spiritual blindness at that memory. Your enemy wants to restrict your sight and give you a fearful spirit. But I want you to see the truth, that you are totally forgiven and deeply loved. Your enemy wants you to live for the present. But I want you to live for eternity. Regardless of your current condition, never forget that I am the One who opens blind eyes. I am the only One who can clear away the floaters, the fog, cataracts, or the total darkness of your mind, body, and spirit. And once you truly see, you will never want to return to the darkness again.

FROM A GRATEFUL HEART
Lord, I've tried unsuccessfully to correct my poor vision. At times, I've even donned rose-colored glasses, unaware or in denial of the truth that lay in front of me. I may never experience physical blindness, but my spirit has often suffered from a lack of discernment, simply because pride, foolishness, or fear overruled good sense and faith. How I thank You for being the One who opens blind eyes. If You hadn't stepped in, darkness would still consume my vision. Because of You, I can now walk in the light. I once was blind, but now, Lord, I see! And the colors of Your love and faithfulness are so bright and clear. Lord, You are the true Sight-giver, and You are the Light.

DAILY TRUTH
At the name of Jesus, darkness always flees.

DAILY REFLECTIONS
"Don't be afraid!" Elisha told him. "For there are more on our side than on theirs!" Then Elisha prayed, "O Lord, open his eyes and let him see!" The Lord opened the young man's eyes, and when he looked up, he saw that the hillside around Elisha was filled with horses and chariots of fire. 2 Kings 6:16-17 NLT

Then Jesus told him, "I have come into the world to give sight to those who are spiritually blind and to show those who think they see that they are blind." John 9:39 TLB

The god of this age has blinded the minds of unbelievers, so that they cannot see the light of the gospel that displays the glory of Christ, who is the image of God. 2 Corinthians 4:4 NIV

But if you don't grow, you are like someone who is nearsighted or blind, and you have forgotten that your past sins are forgiven. 2 Peter 1:9 CEV

DAILY CHALLENGE
Have you ever experienced false guilt? Have you ever been depressed? How have those or other times of mental or spiritual anguish felt like blindness? If you know the first verse of the familiar hymn, *Amazing Grace,* sing those words out loud. Then thank God for opening your "blind" eyes and restoring your sight.

DAILY THOUGHTS & PRAYERS

Day 37

When It Seems God Is Sleeping
The One Who Never Sleeps

*He won't let you stumble,
your Guardian God won't fall asleep.
Not on your life!
Israel's Guardian will never doze or sleep.*
Psalm 121:3-4 MSG

FROM YOUR FAITHFUL FATHER'S HEART
My child, you are never out of My sight. Does that comfort you or frighten you? Sometimes you interpret My silence as absence. But I'm always there with you. Twenty-four hours a day, I watch over My creation. My eyes never close, and My heart is ever tender toward the ones I love. I am the One who never sleeps. Not once will you ever catch Me dozing. No one ever surprises Me. As your Guardian, your Creator, and your faithful Father, I have a vested interest in everything you do. In this lifetime you will never know how many times I've protected you and kept your enemy from harming you. I see every action, hear every word, and know every motive of your heart. I'm aware of every thought you think. And I still love you, just as you are.

FROM A GRATEFUL HEART
Lord, I confess there were times when I interpreted Your silence as if You were sleeping. My life is like an open book to You. Some pages I'd like to rip out, but in Your grace, You've destroyed them and rewritten new ones. You've offered me new opportunities to love and serve You. You've seen me at my worst, yet You love me with all my faults, and You work with me to pull out the best buried deep within my heart. I remember some late-night sessions with You as I poured out my heart. Tears formed rivers down my cheeks, and my eyes refused to close. In those times, I've been so grateful You are the One who never sleeps. You guard my steps and provide angel

protection all around me. Praise You, Father!

DAILY TRUTH
The God who never sleeps is always on call.

DAILY REFLECTIONS
*G*OD*, investigate my life; get all the facts firsthand. I'm an open book to you; even from a distance, you know what I'm thinking. You know when I leave and when I get back; I'm never out of your sight. You know everything I'm going to say before I start the first sentence. I look behind me and you're there, then up ahead and you're there, too—your reassuring presence, coming and going. This is too much, too wonderful—I can't take it all in! Psalm 139:1-6 MSG*

*The angel of the L*ORD *encamps around those who fear him, and he delivers them. Psalm 34:7 NIV*

*The L*ORD *is like a father to his children, tender and compassionate to those who fear him. Psalm 103:13 NLT*

We know how much God loves us because we have felt his love and because we believe him when he tells us that he loves us dearly. God is love, and anyone who lives in love is living with God and God is living in him. 1 John 4:16 TLB

DAILY CHALLENGE
Think about any close calls in your life, times when you or any family members escaped harm. Take a moment to thank God for His protection during those experiences. Find a blank sheet of paper. Today, let that clean paper represent your life. Offer it to God and ask Him to write on your heart anything He wants.

DAILY THOUGHTS & PRAYERS

Day 38

When You Crave God's Blessings
The One Who Gives You Every Spiritual Blessing

Every spiritual blessing in the heavenly realm has already been lavished upon us as a love gift from our wonderful heavenly Father, the Father of our Lord Jesus— all because he sees us wrapped into Christ. This is why we celebrate him with all our hearts!
Ephesians 1:3 TPT

FROM YOUR FAITHFUL FATHER'S HEART
My child, as the One who blesses you with every spiritual blessing, I've planned so much for you. I've given you an inheritance filled with good gifts that will last forever. You may think of blessings as earthly treasures, minimal pain, or the absence of negative circumstances here on earth. But My spiritual blessings have no equal. My gifts are precious things you must unwrap: forgiveness and salvation, joy for your life, a grace-filled, sweet relationship with Me, and a meaningful purpose that will bring glory to My name. I've secured your future home in heaven, and My signature is on every spiritual blessing heaven allows for you, too many for you to ever enumerate. A shower of good and perfect gifts has always been yours— from the moment I adopted you as My child. But you must unwrap them and receive them by faith.

FROM A GRATEFUL HEART
Father, I can't wrap my mind around Your words. You are the One who blesses me with every spiritual blessing. Yet what does that involve? You are so good and wise and wonderful. Why would You want to bless someone like me? Though I'll never understand all You mean by spiritual blessing, I'm beginning to see. Along with the tangible gifts of home, friends, family—and so much more—You have redeemed me, restored me, and forgiven me completely. You have blessed me with inexpressible joy, a deep settled peace, a sense of belonging, a purpose for living, and eternal security found

only in You through Christ. I thank You, Lord, for undeserved blessings in the past, and for a future inheritance that will last.

DAILY TRUTH
When it comes to blessing His children, God is never stingy.

DAILY REFLECTIONS
"If you, imperfect as you are, know how to lovingly take care of your children and give them what's best, how much more ready is your heavenly Father to give wonderful gifts to those who ask him?" Matthew 7:11 TPT

Every good and perfect gift is from above, coming down from the Father of the heavenly lights, who does not change like shifting shadows. James 1:17 NIV

You love him even though you have never seen him. Though you do not see him now, you trust him; and you rejoice with a glorious, inexpressible joy. 1 Peter 1:8 NLT

Praise be to the God and Father of our Lord Jesus Christ! In his great mercy he has given us new birth into a living hope through the resurrection of Jesus Christ from the dead, and into an inheritance that can never perish, spoil or fade. This inheritance is kept in heaven for you, who through faith are shielded by God's power until the coming of the salvation that is ready to be revealed in the last time. 1 Peter 1:3-5 NIV

DAILY CHALLENGE

Make a list of both tangible and intangible things you would consider as blessings (food, shelter, job, friends, laughter, flowers, family, etc.) Now think of every spiritual blessing God has promised. How many can you name? Write those down. Why do you think God wants to give those gifts to you? What is His condition for receiving them? Give God thanks for all His blessings.

DAILY THOUGHTS & PRAYERS

Day 39

When You Desperately Need God's Help
The One Who Is Ready to Help You

*God is our refuge and strength,
always ready to help in times of trouble.*
Psalm 46:1 NLT

FROM YOUR FAITHFUL FATHER'S HEART
My child, I've not left you alone in your helplessness. Trouble will find you, but I will be your refuge and strength in those times. My plan has been clear and available to all who want to seek Me and know Me. I have reconciled the world to Myself. I have placed a bridge over the impossible and impassable chasm between us. My Son Jesus is that bridge, and it is through Him and His sacrifice that all can come into My presence and into My fellowship, just as you have learned to do. I am the One who is ready to help you and anyone who calls on My name. Remember that your need and desperation ushers in My faithfulness to deliver you when you call on Me. No matter what you are going through, I will be with you. Use your need—and My help—to give you the motivation to warn others, My child. Today is the day for them to turn to Me. Tomorrow may never come. Procrastination could end in despair and eternal separation. My Spirit continues to draw others to Myself, but the time is now. Let others know of My faithfulness to help in times of trouble.

FROM A GRATEFUL HEART
Lord, how I need You! Desperation fills my heart, stifling the breath of Your Spirit. I cry out to You because I remember Your promises to help in times of trouble. No matter what has come against me, You've always been there. I can count on Your faithfulness. So here I am once again with no place to turn but to You. I refuse to give up. Thank You for Your salvation, and for giving me the courage and strength to be Your ambassador. Fill me with fresh boldness to encourage others. Sometimes I talk, but others won't

listen. Sometimes I plead, but they won't heed. Lord, You are the One who is ready to help. When I was unlovely, stubborn, and proud, You pursued me and loved me into Your family. You didn't force me, but You showed me the way to salvation. You now see me as Your faultless child. I no longer dread the future. Instead, I welcome Your Spirit's interference and leading in my life. Just as You helped me find the way, I want to help others find Jesus, who is the Way, the Truth, and the Life.

DAILY TRUTH
Trying to live on our own results in living alone—and apart from the only One who can help.

DAILY REFLECTIONS
For God says, "At just the right time, I heard you. On the day of salvation, I helped you." Indeed, the "right time" is now. Today is the day of salvation. 2 Corinthians 6:2 NLT

Yet now he has reconciled you to himself through the death of Christ in his physical body. As a result, he has brought you into his own presence, and you are holy and blameless as you stand before him without a single fault. Colossians 1:22 NLT

Jesus answered, "I am the way and the truth and the life. No one comes to the Father except through me." John 14:6 NIV

But the Lord will be the Savior of all who love him. Even in their time of trouble God will live in them as strength. Psalm 37:39 TPT

DAILY CHALLENGE
When has God been a refuge and strength for you? How do you need His help today? List three people you know who desperately need God's help or His salvation. Pray for them by name each day.

DAILY THOUGHTS & PRAYERS

Day 40

When You've Wandered Away
The One Who Will Heal Your Wayward Heart

"My wayward children," says the Lord,
"come back to me, and I will heal your wayward hearts."
Jeremiah 3:22 NLT

FROM YOUR FAITHFUL FATHER'S HEART

My child, read My words. Hear My heart. I want to meet your needs. Even though you may turn away or betray Me, I will not leave you. I hear your cries. I see your wanderings, and I know what will fill your life. You've tried so many substitutes, searching for something or someone to satisfy your longings. But I'm the only One who can. You are like a prodigal who ignores My calls. When you do that, you suffer from the deception of your choices, while forgetting that I am your faithful Father. I have already forgiven you. I am waiting for you with open arms. You are My child forever, and I am passionate about My love for you. Come back to Me, and receive the inheritance that is yours because of the price I paid for you. You cannot run far from Me. I am the God who made your heart, and I am the One who will heal it if you will let Me. My love and compassion will always be there for you because I am the One who heals wayward hearts.

FROM A GRATEFUL HEART

Lord, I feel like a prodigal who strayed from Your presence and stayed away far too long. I searched for independence but found only bondage. I wanted success but earned only failure. Every avenue I chose brought only heartache and sadness. The stench of garbage clings to my flesh and my clothes, and I don't know where to go or what to do. But Lord, I'm tired of running. Lead me back to Your amazing grace. You've promised that no sin is too great to be forgiven, and no pain is too deep to be healed. I deserve nothing, but I'm confessing my deep need for You. Only You can restore me and save me from the foolishness of my actions. Heavenly Father, You are the only One who can heal my wayward heart. Like a prodigal returning to a loving father, I am coming home to You. I am running to Your arms again.

DAILY TRUTH
You can never run so far that God cannot reach you.

DAILY REFLECTIONS
For the wisdom of the wise will keep life on the right track, while the fool only deceives himself and refuses to face reality. Proverbs 14:8 TPT

When the righteous cry for help, the Lord hears and delivers them out of all their troubles. Psalm 34:17 ESV

I've blotted out your sins; they are gone like morning mist at noon! Oh, return to me, for I have paid the price to set you free. Isaiah 44:22 TLB

As a father has compassion on his children, so the Lord has compassion on those who fear him; for he knows how we are formed, he remembers that we are dust. Psalm 103:13-14 NIV

DAILY CHALLENGE
Read the parable of the lost son (prodigal) in Luke 15:11-31. How would you describe the father? The lost son? How does the father treat his lost son when he returns home? What is Jesus trying to tell us here about our heavenly Father? How does that make you feel? Do you know any prodigals? If so, list their names, and commit to pray for them often.

DAILY THOUGHTS & PRAYERS

Day 41

When You Need Order in Your Life
The One Who Rules Over Everything

*The Lord has made the heavens his throne;
from there he rules over everything there is.
Bless the Lord, you mighty angels of his who carry out his orders,
listening for each of his commands.*
Psalm 103:19-20 TLB

FROM YOUR FAITHFUL FATHER'S HEART
My child, I created everything in perfect order. Why should you worry about things out of your control? You can't fix or control others or the unexpected events in your life. I am still the One who rules over everything and everyone, and I determined My plans for your life long before your birth. I know exactly what you need. If angels, always listening for My voice, act as obedient messengers for Me, why wouldn't you trust Me to orchestrate your life? Not a single creature escapes My rule or attention. I am the King of Kings and Lord of Lords. You can trust My leadership. Rest in the knowledge that I am on My throne, and that I am totally in charge of everything that goes on in your life—and in My entire world.

FROM A GRATEFUL HEART
Lord, I don't understand the messiness in my life, the times when nothing seems to go right. I order my day; but before long, it orders me. Then I see chaos in the world: hatred still divides; crime runs rampant; diseases steal lives, and natural disasters destroy entire communities. Yet nothing surprises You. You are still the One who created all things and who rules over everything. I am so glad You are in charge. Order my steps, Lord, and give me discernment to live each day wisely. One day You will usher in a new heaven and a new earth, and sin will no longer contaminate Your creation. I look forward to that time of restored perfection. Thank You for being my Father and my God. You are the Lord of my life, and I choose to trust You

and Your perfect system of order.

DAILY TRUTH
With God on His throne, we're never alone.

DAILY REFLECTIONS
You saw me before I was born. Every day of my life was recorded in your book. Every moment was laid out before a single day had passed. Psalm 139:16 NLT

"Remember, your Father knows exactly what you need even before you ask him!" Matthew 6:8 TLB

By faith—by believing God—we know that the world and the stars—in fact, all things—were made at God's command; and that they were all made from things that can't be seen. Hebrews 11:3 TLB

But the Eternal has not moved; He remains in His holy temple. He sits squarely on His heavenly throne. He observes the sons of Adam and daughters of Eve, examining us within and without, exploring every fiber of our beings. Psalm 11:4 VOICE

DAILY CHALLENGE
Make two columns on a sheet of paper. List the things you can control (attitude, choices, etc.) on one side. Now write down what you can't control in the other column. Place a big X over the second column, and release those things to God. Place a big checkmark across the first column. Ask God to help you make wise and positive decisions about the things listed there. If it helps, review the words to the popular *Serenity Prayer*.

DAILY THOUGHTS & PRAYERS

Day 42

When You Need Assurance You Are God's Child
The One Who Whispers Reassurance to You

> *For the Holy Spirit makes God's fatherhood real to us*
> *as he whispers into our innermost being,*
> *"You are God's beloved child!"*
> Romans 8:16 TPT

FROM YOUR FAITHFUL FATHER'S HEART
My child, do you still question at times if you are a child of Mine? Where are those doubts coming from? Are you being led by My Spirit or your own emotions? Your relationship with Me doesn't depend on your feelings but your faith in Me. Your enemy will not only attack you with doubts about My faithfulness; he wants to destroy you and your assurance. Your part? Receive My words and believe them. If you have confessed Me as Lord and Savior of your life and have chosen to accept My sacrificial death as the payment for your sin, then by faith you are My child. You receive all the rights, privileges, and responsibilities that accompany that relationship. Your name is on a heavenly birth certificate signed with My blood. I have filled you with My Holy Spirit not only to confirm your relationship with Me but also to make you a bold disciple of Mine. I am the One who whispers reassurance to you through the power of My Spirit. I have planned so much for you as My child. You have freedom—and power—to follow Me!

FROM A GRATEFUL HEART
Lord, sometimes it's hard for me to understand our relationship. Being adopted into Your family, making me Your child—I admit that blows me away. My weaknesses glare at me like a warped mirror. I am so not like You. But then Your Holy Spirit speaks to my spirit that I am indeed Yours and that I truly am Your child. I am so glad You are the One who whispers reassurance to me. You constantly prod me, teach me, and lead me in the way I should go. You don't stand far off, leaving me to fend for myself. You

are a perfect Father—always near, always loving me, and always drawing me to Yourself. Thank You, Lord!

DAILY TRUTH
God never speaks anything but the truth, the whole truth, and nothing but the truth.

DAILY REFLECTIONS
But to all who believed him and accepted him, he gave the right to become children of God. John 1:12 NLT

If the Spirit of God is leading you, then take comfort in knowing you are His children. Romans 8:14 VOICE

So in Christ Jesus you are all children of God through faith. Galatians 3:26 NIV

For if you tell others with your own mouth that Jesus Christ is your Lord and believe in your own heart that God has raised him from the dead, you will be saved. For it is by believing in his heart that a man becomes right with God; and with his mouth he tells others of his faith, confirming his salvation. Romans 10:9-10 TLB

DAILY CHALLENGE
Draw a line down the middle of a page. On one side, using adjectives, how would you describe a perfect father? On the other side, list the attributes of your perfect heavenly Father. Thank God today that He loves you, that you are truly His child, and that He is the perfect Father to you.

DAILY THOUGHTS & PRAYERS

Day 43

When You Want Freedom from Sin's Control
The One Who Offers Freedom

Sin can't tell you how to live.
After all, you're not living under that old tyranny any longer.
You're living in the freedom of God.
Romans 6:14 MSG

FROM YOUR FAITHFUL FATHER'S HEART
My child, because you belong to Me, I have given you freedom from sin's power—freedom to live for Me. My grace now motivates you, not the obligation of your old nature. As long as you lived under sin's control, your old nature, you lived like a prisoner bound by chains. But as My forgiven child, those constraints have been broken. Has someone or something tried to pull you into bondage again? Are old habits trying to gain an entrance into your heart? Consider yourself dead to those impulses. Why would you want to revert to the grip of sin instead of living under My grace? Do you long for true freedom? My death guaranteed that for you. My power is always available to you, and it will give you victory over sin. I am the One who offers freedom. Like a butterfly released from the spider's web, you are free, My child. Spread your wings and fly.

FROM A GRATEFUL HEART
Lord, I am free—really free. Those words spark hope in my heart each time I am tempted to doubt or make a wrong decision. Why would I want to return to a life of bondage? Sin no longer has any permanent hold on me. You placed a new desire in my heart to live for You. Because of Your death and power over sin, I, too, can experience victory. The whispers of my enemy fade as I listen to You, the One who offers freedom. Your grace is enough to keep me moving ahead in humility and gratitude. My performance won't be perfect. But even when I do sin, Your forgiveness is there for me. I owe You so much! The constant desire of my heart is to obey You and follow

You wherever You take me.

DAILY TRUTH
God's gift of grace releases us from the grip of sin.

DAILY REFLECTIONS
So here is how to picture yourself now that you have been initiated into Jesus the Anointed: you are dead to sin's power and influence, but you are alive to God's rule. Romans 6:11 VOICE

But the Scriptures declare that we are all prisoners of sin, so we receive God's promise of freedom only by believing in Jesus Christ. Galatians 3:22 NLT

At last we have freedom, for Christ has set us free! We must always cherish this truth and firmly refuse to go back into the bondage of our past. Galatians 5:1 TPT

Yet God, in his grace, freely makes us right in his sight. He did this through Christ Jesus when he freed us from the penalty for our sins. Romans 3:24 NLT

DAILY CHALLENGE
How do you think most people define freedom? What is your definition? What does it mean to you? Think about a time when you didn't experience freedom, or at least you didn't understand it. How has that changed through the years? Are there any areas of your life in which you still desire God's freedom? Spend a few moments in prayer expressing your need and asking God for deliverance.

DAILY THOUGHTS & PRAYERS

Day 44

When Your Work Seems Small
The One Who Makes the Seed Grow

*I planted the seed in your hearts, and Apollos watered it,
but it was God who made it grow.*
1 Corinthians 3:6 NLT

FROM YOUR FAITHFUL FATHER'S HEART
My child, I assign tasks to all of My children. To some, I give the seeds of faith to plant into the fertile soil of another's heart. I commission others to add life-giving water to the thirsty spirit. Should My children argue about which one is more important? Neither one pushes that seed through to maturity. I am the One who makes the seed grow. We are all a team, working together for My purpose. Every act of kindness, every deed of love, and every word about Me is like a seed planted in another's heart. To have a part—any role—in growing My kingdom is both a privilege and an honor. No assignment is too small. And none is more important than the other. Like the little boy who offered his lunch to Me on the Judean hillside one day to feed over 5,000, you, too, will see your gifts—and work—multiplied. Whether you are a seed planter or one who waters, you will share in the fruit of your labor, and others will come to know Me.

FROM A GRATEFUL HEART
Father, my work seems so small and unimportant at times. Yet You assure me that it's valuable. Thank You for trusting me with Your kingdom work. Whatever my assignment, I want to do it well and bring You honor and glory. Whether I speak a word of truth or personal testimony or share the rich message of salvation with someone, You allow me the joy of partnering with You and others to help Your family grow. I may not see the fruit of that planted seed or the results of watering it in my lifetime, but one day You will unveil the truth—and the outcome. Then we will know and celebrate both the joy of serving You and seeing the full-grown plant: another

child added to Your wonderful family.

DAILY TRUTH
Growing is God's business. Planting is ours.

DAILY REFLECTIONS
"Plant the good seeds of righteousness, and you will reap a crop of my love." Hosea 10:12 TLB

It's not important who does the planting, or who does the watering. What's important is that God makes the seed grow. The one who plants and the one who waters work together with the same purpose. And both will be rewarded for their own hard work. 1 Corinthians 3:7-8 NLT

"Here is a boy with five small barley loaves and two small fish, but how far will they go among so many?" John 6:9 NIV

Now the One who provides seed for the sower and bread for food will provide and multiply your seed and increase the harvest of your righteousness. 2 Corinthians 9:10 HCSB

DAILY CHALLENGE
Have you ever tried to grow vegetables or flowers? Did you plant seeds, or did you transplant what someone else had already planted? What would have happened if you didn't water that plant? Ask God to help you complete any tasks He wants to give you: to plant the seed of encouragement in someone's life, to share a positive word from Scripture or your testimony, to pray for them, or to tell someone how they can become a child of God, using strategic Bible verses.

DAILY THOUGHTS & PRAYERS

Day 45

When You Call Yourself a Nobody
The One Who Uses Nobodies

*Isn't it obvious that God deliberately chose men and women
that the culture overlooks and exploits and abuses,
chose these "nobodies" to expose the hollow pretensions
of the "somebodies"?*
1 Corinthians 1:27 MSG

FROM YOUR FAITHFUL FATHER'S HEART
My child, sometimes you call yourself a "nobody." Do you envy the ten-talent achiever, the rich and famous, or the ones who boast of their self-made success? I chose David, a simple shepherd boy, to rule over a nation. I used an ordinary, young woman named Mary, a virgin, to birth My own Son. I entrusted a dozen "nobodies" as disciples to impact My world. I don't look at the outside; I see what's in the heart. The very ones you may call insignificant are at the top of My most useable list. That way, pride never gets in the way. I design a special purpose for all My children, rich or poor, multi or single talented, famous or anonymous. But the purpose of all My creation is to bring Me glory. I love to take your faithfulness in little things to create a powerful man or woman for My use. I am the One who chooses—and uses—nobodies and makes them somebodies in My kingdom.

FROM A GRATEFUL HEART
Lord, I look in the mirror and see the word *nobody* written in imaginary letters. Yet I am so grateful You superimposed the words *My Somebody* in red letters on that mirror. At times my journey with You has been breathtaking, like a roller coaster at an amusement park. Other times I've felt so ordinary, stuck in the ruts of my doubts. But I'm so glad You are the One who uses *nobodies*. You turn my weakness into strength, and the impossible into possibilities. Thank You for reminding me often that You love to use followers like me—in big and small ways—to make a difference in Your

world. Thank You for designing me with special care and love. How I long to bring You honor, praise, and glory, Lord!

DAILY TRUTH
God delights in turning nobodies into somebodies for Him.

DAILY REFLECTIONS
"The LORD does not look at the things people look at. People look at the outward appearance, but the LORD looks at the heart." 1 Samuel 16:7 NIV

When they saw the courage of Peter and John and realized that they were unschooled, ordinary men, they were astonished and they took note that these men had been with Jesus. Acts 4:13 NIV

This is how Jesus the Messiah was born. His mother, Mary, was engaged to be married to Joseph. But before the marriage took place, while she was still a virgin, she became pregnant through the power of the Holy Spirit. Matthew 1:18 NLT

I'll call nobodies and make them somebodies; I'll call the unloved and make them beloved. In the place where they yelled out, "You're nobody!" they're calling you "God's living children." Romans 9:25-26 MSG

DAILY CHALLENGE
As a reminder for today, write on a hand mirror or bathroom mirror with shaving cream or something easily cleanable: "I am God's Somebody." Then thank God for making you His special somebody. (Don't forget to clean the mirror later).

DAILY THOUGHTS & PRAYERS

Day 46

When You Need a Promise Keeper
The One Who Always Keeps His Promises

For your kingdom is an everlasting kingdom.
You rule throughout all generations.
*The L*ORD *always keeps his promises;*
he is gracious in all he does.
Psalm 145:13 NLT

FROM YOUR FAITHFUL FATHER'S HEART
My child, I have given you everything you need to live for Me: boldness, strength, wisdom, giftedness, and so much more. Whether you receive and apply them is up to you. Because you belong to Me, I will never leave you to fend for yourself on this wonderful adventure of life. I am still faithful; I am the One who always keeps His promises in every generation. Are you doubting Me? Search for My promises; trust My timing; cultivate faithfulness, and then wait patiently for Me to work in your life and the lives of others as you join Me on your journey. Keep doing good and feed on Me. I have called you for My purpose, and when you look to Me for every provision, you will find everything you need. When I return for you and all My children one day, what a joy you will experience to hear My "well done." I will help you remain faithful until the end.

FROM A GRATEFUL HEART
Lord, I want to keep my word, but I fail so often. You are the One—the only One—who always keeps His promises, the God who faithfully does what He says. I'm the one who has created gaps in my faithfulness to You. And yet You continually demonstrate Your goodness in my life. Every word You speak is truth, and I can document the results of Your faithfulness to those promises. I'm so eager to serve You. Thank You for the gifts You've given me, for never giving up on me, and for constantly assuring me that You will finish the work You started in me—until the day You return.

DAILY TRUTH
God says what He means, and means what He says.

DAILY REFLECTIONS
You are not ill-equipped or slighted on any necessary gifts as you patiently anticipate the day when our Lord Jesus, the Anointed One, is revealed. Until that final day, He will preserve you; and on that day, He will consider you faultless. Count on this: God is faithful and in His faithfulness called you out into an intimate relationship with His Son, our Lord Jesus the Anointed. 1 Corinthians 1:7-9 VOICE

"He will always give you all you need from day to day if you will make the Kingdom of God your primary concern." Luke 12:31 TLB

Trust in the Lord and do good; Live in the land and cultivate faithfulness. Psalm 37:3 NASB

"O Lord God of Israel, there is no God like you in all of heaven and earth. You are the God who keeps his kind promises to all those who obey you and who are anxious to do your will." 2 Chronicles 6:14 TLB

DAILY CHALLENGE
What promises has God kept in your life? Begin a small notebook, file, or folder and label it "God's promises." As you take time to read the Bible each day, watch for His promises in Scripture and record them in your file or notebook. Each week, meditate on a new promise you find. Consider memorizing those that are especially meaningful to you.

DAILY THOUGHTS & PRAYERS

Day 47

When You Need Courage
The One Who Makes You Strong

All of our praise rises to the One who is strong enough to make you strong, exactly as preached in Jesus Christ, precisely as revealed in the mystery kept secret for so long but now an open book through the prophetic Scriptures. All the nations of the world can now know the truth and be brought into obedient belief, carrying out the orders of God, who got all this started, down to the final detail.
Romans 16:25-26 MSG

FROM YOUR FAITHFUL FATHER'S HEART
My child, when others try to shake your faith, question your motives, or destroy your influence, remember that I am the One who makes you strong. Watch out for those who act deceitfully. Guard yourself and those you love from the ones who care more for themselves and their agendas than for My message of love and salvation. But remember I died for everyone. Let My example temper your emotions and give you self-control. I have not given you a spirit of fear. You can speak to others with boldness and confidence as I fill you with My Spirit. Be gentle and listen to others. But always be ready to give a reason for the hope that is growing within you. Let your love for Me override any hesitancy or fear. I will honor what you do in My name and will give you the strength to keep sharing My truth not only with humility and grace but also in My power. How others respond is not your concern. Always leave the results to Me.

FROM A GRATEFUL HEART
Lord, sometimes my stomach turns to jelly in the presence of unbelievers or those who dishonor Your name. I forget about depending on You and start focusing on my inadequacies. You are the One who makes me strong. You are the One who overshadows my timidity with the boldness of Your Spirit. Your message is more important than my comfort. I care about oth-

ers because Your love compels me to reach out in love. Help me to listen more and then to speak up at Your Spirit's prompting. I release my fears and shortcomings into Your hands, Lord. Thank You for Your strength and courage.

DAILY TRUTH
When our strength is gone, God is the One we can still count on.

DAILY REFLECTIONS
Be on your guard; stand firm in the faith; be courageous; be strong. 1 Corinthians 16:13 NIV

For the Spirit God gave us does not make us timid, but gives us power, love and self-discipline. 2 Timothy 1:7 NIV

"Those who honor me I will honor." 1 Samuel 2:30 NIV

But instead we will remain strong and always sincere in our love as we express the truth. All our direction and ministries will flow from Christ and lead us deeper into him, the anointed Head of his body, the church. Ephesians 4:15 TPT

DAILY CHALLENGE
Memorize 2 Timothy 1:7. Write down the names of three friends who need God's loving touch on their lives. Pray for them, and ask God to give you an opportunity and the boldness this week to share His love with at least one of those three people or with someone else the Lord may lay on your heart.

DAILY THOUGHTS & PRAYERS

Day 48

When You Struggle with Motives
The One Who Examines All Motives

*For we speak as messengers approved by God
to be entrusted with the Good News.
Our purpose is to please God, not people.
He alone examines the motives of our hearts.*
1 Thessalonians 2:4 NLT

FROM YOUR FAITHFUL FATHER'S HEART
My child, if you are seeking to be a God pleaser, not a people pleaser, I will be faithful to verify your message and your mission. Flattery attempts to please others, not Me. People are looking for authenticity in My children. Some may criticize your life and your efforts and question your motives. When you constantly ask Me to show you anything hurtful to yourself or Me, I will reveal it. But be prepared. I am the One who examines all motives. I will right the wrongs one day of those who refused My grace and love and of those who tried to hurt My children. I know the state of your heart. It can be deceitful, and you must guard it at all costs. In everything you do or say, do it for My glory. Then your motives will reflect My heart and My will, and My message will accomplish what I want it to.

FROM A GRATEFUL HEART
Lord, I confess my weakness when I've inflated my importance, temporarily forgetting my true identity in Christ. As a child of God, I belong to You. I owe everything to You. My heart's desire, Lord, is to follow You faithfully, no matter what the cost. I'm so glad that You are the God who examines all motives. Because I am still human, I know my motives are never completely pure. Sometimes I try to defend my preferences and opinions as if they were convictions. And at times I'm tempted to amend my convictions to avoid controversy. But I long for a heart that is completely true to You. Thank You for Your patience with me. Help me to be patient with myself.

You created me. You know my heart better than I ever could. Help me, Lord, to always be a God pleaser.

DAILY TRUTH
Schmoozing can lead to snoozing. Stay alert. Be a God pleaser.

DAILY REFLECTIONS
You can see that I am not trying to please you by sweet talk and flattery; no, I am trying to please God. If I were still trying to please men I could not be Christ's servant. Galatians 1:10 TLB

We are all in love with our own opinions, convinced they're correct. But the Lord is in the midst of us, testing and probing our every motive. Proverbs 16:2 TPT

"The human heart is the most deceitful of all things, and desperately wicked. Who really knows how bad it is? But I, the Lord, search all hearts and examine secret motives. I give all people their due rewards, according to what their actions deserve." Jeremiah 17:9-10 NLT

And whatever you do, whether in word or deed, do it all in the name of the Lord Jesus, giving thanks to God the Father through him. Colossians 3:17 NIV

DAILY CHALLENGE
Do you ever struggle with impure motives? What can you do to avoid being a people pleaser? Every morning when you awake, pray the words of Psalm 51:10 in any translation you choose. Here is that prayer in The Living Bible (TLB): *Create in me a new, clean heart, O God, filled with clean thoughts and right desires.*

DAILY THOUGHTS & PRAYERS

Day 49

When You Feel God Doesn't Need You
The One Who Has No Needs

"He is the God who made the world and everything in it.
Since he is Lord of heaven and earth,
he doesn't live in man-made temples,
and human hands can't serve his needs—for he has no needs.
He himself gives life and breath to everything,
and he satisfies every need."
Acts 17:24-25 NLT

FROM YOUR FAITHFUL FATHER'S HEART
My child, you work so hard to serve Me. And I want your willing service. But I don't need your help. Does that surprise you? I am the One who has no needs. I am self-existent and completely self-sufficient. I cannot be anyone but who I am. I am the Alpha and Omega. Before you, I was. Before the world existed, I was. I will always be the great *I Am*. And I am still the One who gives life to every being, the God who set the world on its axis, and the God who controls everything. You can never completely understand those things in this world. But you can trust Me. Why would I need human help? Even though I have no needs, I want you. I love you so much that I want you to be a part of My family. I chose to give you meaningful work, and I desire your fellowship daily.

FROM A GRATEFUL HEART
Lord, joy and gratitude well up in my heart every morning when I awake and realize You want me as Your child. Nothing surprises You; nothing catches You off guard. You are never hungry, thirsty, or tired. You are the One who has no needs. I know You are not here for me, just to make me happy. But I want to be here for You, Lord. Nothing brings me more pleasure than to worship You and to love You with all that I am. Thank You for allowing me to have a part in Your kingdom's work. You may not need me,

but You love my praise. You love it when I love You. And I do love You, Lord. Thank You for wanting me, for choosing me, and for designing such a wonderful plan for the ones You created. I love being a part of Your creation. And I love being Your child.

DAILY TRUTH
The God who has no needs still wants you, loves you, and delights in you.

DAILY REFLECTIONS
In the beginning God created the heavens and the earth. Genesis 1:1 NIV

And he also said, "It is finished! I am the Alpha and the Omega—the Beginning and the End. To all who are thirsty I will give freely from the springs of the water of life." Revelation 21:6 NLT

God replied to Moses, "I AM WHO I AM." Exodus 3:14 NLT

God is faithful, through whom you were called into fellowship with His Son, Jesus Christ our Lord. 1 Corinthians 1:9 NASB

DAILY CHALLENGE
Today in your prayer time, spend several minutes praising our triune God for who He is. Think about His names, maybe some you have read in this devotional, and others you can find in His Word. Try going through the alphabet: "Lord, I praise You for being my Abba Father, the Beloved, my Comforter." "Thank You that You are my Everlasting Father, my Friend, and the Good Shepherd." If it helps, write down those names to remember each time you pray.

DAILY THOUGHTS & PRAYERS

Day 50

When You Need to Forgive Yourself
The One Who Forgives Completely

*"I, yes I, am the One and Only, who completely erases your sins,
never to be seen again. I will not remember them again.
Freely I do this because of who I am!"*
Isaiah 43:25 TPT

FROM YOUR FAITHFUL FATHER'S HEART

My child, why are you still wrestling with sin and rebellion from your past? In your mind, sin lingers like the bad aftertaste of bitter fruit. You can't forget what happened. And you have difficulty forgiving yourself. You approach Me, repentant, begging for forgiveness again. For what? I already forgave you long ago, My child. I removed your sins from you as far as the east is from the west. How can I do that? Because I am still the One who forgives completely, the One who erases all your sin and shame. You may reap some natural consequences for your actions, but I will give you grace to live for Me. You can never pay enough for your sin. I already did that. I paid the one-time penalty when I died on the cross for you. I choose to no longer hold sin to your account. Instead, remember My words: "Leave your life of sin." Your enemy wants to plant shame in your heart. But My forgiveness is complete: past, present, and future. You are free from the power of sin's grip. Receive it joyfully. That grace set you free. And My grace will keep you close to Me.

FROM A GRATEFUL HEART

Lord, nothing about You is "sometimes." Your love, Your grace, and yes, Your forgiveness is complete. Thank You for not allowing my past to define me. I will never understand why You treat me as Your beloved child instead of the fickle follower I am. I can never truly forget my sins. Yet You forget and forgive them. I fail You repeatedly, yet You continue to love and accept me. Something changed, though, when I chose to follow You. The desire to disobey continues to fade with the realization that You are the One who forgives me completely. To wake up each morning knowing I am forgiven, accepted, and loved, and that You will give me the strength to face whatever comes—that kind of love and acceptance compels me to live for You daily. From now on, my motto will read, "no guilt, no regrets; only grace and gratitude." Thank You for Your complete forgiveness and amazing grace, Lord!

DAILY TRUTH
God erases our sins, but never His forgiveness.

DAILY REFLECTIONS
Since we are now joined to Christ, we have been given the treasures of redemption by his blood—the total cancellation of our sins—all because of the cascading riches of his grace. Ephesians 1:7 TPT

Do not be deceived, God is not mocked; for whatever a person sows, this he will also reap. Galatians 6:7 NASB

"Then neither do I condemn you," Jesus declared. "Go now and leave your life of sin." John 8:11 NIV

He has removed our sins as far from us as the east is from the west. Psalm 103:12 NLT

DAILY CHALLENGE
Whenever you are tempted to cling to past sins or entertain regretful thoughts about your past, list that sin (or sins). Beside each sin, write GRACE to remind you of God's complete forgiveness. Then place a huge X across the page to signify Jesus' payment for your sin.

DAILY THOUGHTS & PRAYERS

Day 51

When You Need a Shepherd
The One Who Is Your Good Shepherd

*"I alone am the Good Shepherd,
and I know those whose hearts are mine,
for they recognize me and know me,
just as my Father knows my heart and I know my Father's heart.
I am ready to give my life for the sheep."*
John 10:14-15 TPT

FROM YOUR FAITHFUL FATHER'S HEART
My child, when sheep are left alone, they stray easily. They can even plunge over a cliff by following a fellow, misguided sheep. Because you are like one of those sheep, you also need a shepherd, someone to guide you on the right path. I am the One who is your Good Shepherd. I will provide for you and give you everything you need. As the One who shepherds you, I know your weaknesses and your tendencies to head off in the wrong direction. Gently but firmly, I will lead you. I have walked those paths previously. I have confronted the darkness. And I will protect you from your enemies. I am always present to rescue you, My child. Nothing and no one can separate you from My love. And no one can snatch you from My hand. As your Good Shepherd, I love you too much to leave you unprotected.

FROM A GRATEFUL HEART
Father, how I need Your guidance in my life. My proud heart and stubborn ways have led me onto the wrong paths too many times. Instead of looking up and following You as my Good Shepherd, I've often chosen a way that left me stranded. But You rescued me and brought me back to green pastures and quiet streams for rest and refreshment. I don't want to ignore Your voice, because You will always lead me in the right direction. Your sweet whispers nudge me close to You where You keep me safe. You even lay down Your life for me to protect me from my dangerous enemies. My

heart longs to follow You all the days of my life. I never want to stray from You again. There is no one like You!

DAILY TRUTH
The greenest pastures are those the Good Shepherd has prepared for you.

DAILY REFLECTIONS
"But the true Shepherd walks right up to the gate, and because the gatekeeper knows who he is, he opens the gate to let him in. And the sheep recognize the voice of the true Shepherd, for he calls his own by name and leads them out, for they belong to him. And when he has brought out all his sheep, he walks ahead of them and they will follow him, for they are familiar with his voice." John 10:2-4 TPT

Because the Lord is my Shepherd, I have everything I need! He lets me rest in the meadow grass and leads me beside the quiet streams. He gives me new strength. He helps me do what honors him the most. Psalm 23:1-3 TLB

"I give to them the gift of eternal life and they will never be lost and no one has the power to snatch them out of my hands. My Father, who has given them to me as his gift, is the mightiest of all, and no one has the power to snatch them from my Father's care." John 10:28-29 TPT

Like sheep you wandered away from God, but now you have returned to your Shepherd, the Guardian of your souls who keeps you safe from all attacks. 1 Peter 2:25 TLB

DAILY CHALLENGE

Read the parable of the lost sheep in Luke 15:3-7. Describe what your life would be like if Jesus hadn't rescued you. For further study, review Psalm 23 and consider memorizing it. Meditate on the words of this psalm and list the benefits that the Shepherd provides for you.

DAILY THOUGHTS & PRAYERS

Day 52

When You Need Someone to Catch Your Tears
The One Who Wipes Away All Tears

> *"He will wipe away all tears from their eyes,*
> *and there shall be no more death,*
> *nor sorrow, nor crying, nor pain.*
> *All of that has gone forever."*
> Revelation 21:4 TLB

FROM YOUR FAITHFUL FATHER'S HEART

My child, you may think no one hears your cries, especially the silent ones. But I do. I not only hear your weeping, but I also feel every sorrow you experience. Remember, I wept too. I've recorded all your tears. I know every drop that falls. But I will do more than listen. I will also comfort you. Your prayerful cries are like perfume to Me, and I hear them all. Your weeping may last for a little while, but joy will come again. In time, I will turn those tears into bottles of joy released deep within your spirit. No one comforts or cares for you like I do. When your heart is breaking, My Spirit will draw you close. I am the One who wipes away your tears. And one day, I will blot them from your eyes forever. Because in that place of sweet forever, you will experience no more death, no more tears, no more sorrow, and no more pain.

FROM A GRATEFUL HEART

Lord, like the psalmist David, sometimes it feels as if the flow of my tears will never end. At night, I've soaked my pillow with prayerful, wet sobs. The losses in this life burrow deep into my soul trying to take up permanent residence. Do You symbolically catch my tears in Your bottle like the ancient mourners who buried those collections in the graves of their friends as a memorial? When I realize that You are the One who will wipe away all tears in my forever home and that You are the One who hears my weeping here on earth, I can make it through those painful seasons of my life. It's

Your love that's unending, not my tears. You collect my tears and prayers and turn them into a fragrant offering. Without You, I couldn't make it through the day or even through the hour. Knowing that You are that kind of personal God—the only One who listens, hears, comforts, and walks beside me in every season of my life, loving me constantly through the pain—overwhelms me with praise and gratitude. Thank You, Lord! Thank You that in Your presence I can find true joy again and that one day, You will wipe all tears away forever.

DAILY TRUTH
With God, no cry ever goes unheard, and no tears are ever ignored.

DAILY REFLECTIONS
I am worn out from sobbing. All night I flood my bed with weeping, drenching it with my tears. My vision is blurred by grief; my eyes are worn out because of all my enemies. Go away, all you who do evil, for the Lord has heard my weeping. Psalm 6:6-8 NLT

You keep track of all my sorrows. You have collected all my tears in your bottle. You have recorded each one in your book. Psalm 56:8 NLT

And when he had taken it, the four living creatures and the twenty-four elders fell down before the Lamb. Each one had a harp and they were holding golden bowls full of incense, which are the prayers of God's people. Revelation 5:8 NIV

Tears may flow in the night, but joy comes in the morning. Psalm 30:5 GNT

DAILY CHALLENGE
Place a bottle filled with water next to one of your workspaces. Each time you look at that bottle, thank God that He catches and bottles your tears and will one day wipe every tear away.

DAILY THOUGHTS & PRAYERS

Day 53

When Your Heart Cries for Justice
The One Who Gives True Justice

He gives justice to all who are treated unfairly.
Psalm 103:6 TLB

FROM YOUR FAITHFUL FATHER'S HEART
My child, I understand the emotions raging in your heart. Corruption, greed, and injustice live in My world. Everywhere you look today, you'll see the ravages of those who try to steal dignity and life from others. And you've been hurt deeply by the guilty. From the beginning of time, the ones I created chose to rebel against Me, opting for selfish pursuits instead of seeking My heart. Yes, that grieves Me. Yet I am the One responsible for giving justice to all who are treated unfairly, and I am still on My throne. I'm aware of those who have taken unfair advantage of you and all My children. My love is available to all, but all will not choose Me. In this life, you may suffer loss and injustice. The scales may appear to tip the wrong way. And you can work in peaceful ways with honesty and integrity to right the wrongs you see. Do what is right and good, but never choose revenge or violence. I am the One who gives true justice, not you. Revenge belongs to Me, My child.

FROM A GRATEFUL HEART
Lord, none of us like to see bullies, criminals, and corrupt officials prosper in our world. I've cried my share of tears for myself and for innocent ones who have suffered at the hands of ungodly people. And I've tried to stand for right against those who promote wrong. I pray against the evil in our land. But it's Your world. And You are the one in control, not me. I release my right to be right. You see the good and the bad. You know the intentions of every heart. You are the One who gives true justice and the God who is always fair. Those who love darkness will one day experience darkness. But on that day Your children will finally see the light—and the truth.

DAILY TRUTH
God is the One who will right all wrong forever.

DAILY REFLECTIONS
They are people who lack all sense of right and wrong, and who have turned themselves over to doing whatever feels good and to practicing every sort of corruption along with greed. Ephesians 4:19 CEB.

This suffering is all part of the work God has given you. Christ, who suffered for you, is your example. Follow in his steps: He never sinned, never told a lie, never answered back when insulted; when he suffered he did not threaten to get even; he left his case in the hands of God who always judges fairly. 1 Peter 2:21-23 TLB

Beloved, don't be obsessed with taking revenge, but leave that to God's righteous justice. For the Scriptures say: "Vengeance is mine, and I will repay," says the Lord. Romans 12:19 TPT

The Lord has told you what is good. He has told you what he wants from you: Do what is right to other people. Love being kind to others. And live humbly, trusting your God. Micah 6:8 ICB

DAILY CHALLENGE
Release any feelings of revenge you may be experiencing from unfair treatment to you or others. Ask God to fill you with His love. Then as you listen to the news this week, watch for examples of injustice. Pray for those who are suffering, and pray for God to right the wrongs you see. Ask Him to show you how to do what is right, to be kind to others, and to live with a sense of humility.

DAILY THOUGHTS & PRAYERS

Day 54

When You Want a Full Life
The One Who Gives You Life

But each day the LORD *pours his unfailing love upon me,*
and through each night I sing his songs,
praying to God who gives me life.
Psalm 42:8 NLT

FROM YOUR FAITHFUL FATHER'S HEART
My child, do you think I am out to get you? I designed you for My glory. I'm not looking for ways to take you down, but to lift you up. Your enemy wants to prevent you from experiencing all I have planned for you. He will try anything to steal your passion and destroy your hope. But I have set My heart and My unfailing love on you from the day I formed you. Even before that, I drew your blueprints, then gave you your first breath. What kind of life do you want? What does a full life mean to you? Worldly success? Fulfilled ambitions? I am the One who gives you life, but not the kind of meaningless existence that struggles to stay afloat. The life I offer is full, free, and satisfying. The moment you decided to follow Me and accept Me as your Lord, your joy-filled and purpose-filled life began. But it never really ends. One day your physical body will die, but your true spirit—the real you—will then enjoy the full life for which you were created. My child, I created you for eternity—a life that continues forever in My presence.

FROM A GRATEFUL HEART
Lord, thank You for listening to my puny complaints and petty ambitions. You designed me for so much more than that. You are not a God who wants destruction for Your children. You don't condemn us. But we can hurt ourselves by our wrong choices. You are the One who gives me life—a life that goes on forever even after I take my last breath. Teach me what a full life really means, Lord. Help me to be grateful for every moment You give me. I want to spend my days loving You and others more. You pour

Your love on me daily, and I want to give back and share what You have invested in me. Thank You for life, Lord. Today and every day, I sing Your praises.

DAILY TRUTH
Life is a celebration of who God is and whose we are.

DAILY REFLECTIONS
"A thief is only there to steal and kill and destroy. I came so they can have real and eternal life, more and better life than they ever dreamed of." John 10:10 MSG

For you have been born again, but not to a life that will quickly end. Your new life will last forever because it comes from the eternal, living word of God. 1 Peter 1:23 NLT

For You shaped me, inside and out. You knitted me together in my mother's womb long before I took my first breath. Psalm 139:13 VOICE

If you have the Son, you have eternal life. If you do not have the Son of God, you are not acquainted with true life. 1 John 5:12 VOICE

DAILY CHALLENGE
How do these verses bring assurance and satisfaction to you that God wants to give you a full life? In a few sentences, how would you describe to someone who has never had a relationship with Jesus what a full life means to you?

DAILY THOUGHTS & PRAYERS

Day 55

When a Storm Is Brewing
The One Who Calms Your Storms

*But Jesus reprimanded them.
"Why are you gripped with fear? Where is your faith?"
Then he stood up and rebuked the storm and said, "Be still!"
And instantly it became perfectly calm.*
Matthew 8:26 TPT

FROM YOUR FAITHFUL FATHER'S HEART

My child, has fear gripped you once again? You see a storm coming, or maybe you're in the middle of one, and panic is creeping into your heart. What will happen? Your what-ifs are drowning out My whispers to you: "Be still, My child, be still." Examine My track record of faithfulness again. Have I not either delivered you through the storms in your life or walked with you through them? Am I not the Creator of the earth and sky, creatures and seas, and of everything and everyone in the world? Am I not the One who calms the storms? I will also calm your chaos. As I was with My disciples that day on the Sea of Galilee, I will be with you, My child. I know when your faith needs testing. And as you trust in Me, that mustard seed faith will grow bigger. I will guide you safely to a quiet harbor and resting place.

FROM A GRATEFUL HEART

Lord, I sense the beginnings of a storm in my life. I hear the winds howling, threatening to shred my hopes and steal my dreams. Help, Lord! I need Your protection once again. Fear is seeping into the walls of my heart. My faith feels as weak as a newborn kitten. If the waves start foaming and crashing, Lord, would You once again speak peace to the wind and the waves and still my soul? Let me hear Your sweet whispers of love, Lord. You have answered my cries so many times. You never left my side. You either reached down and held me or hushed the winds just when I needed

You the most. Some were storms of my own making, but others caught me unprepared. You are the only One who calms my storms. I want my faith to pass the trust test, Lord. You are indeed worthy of my trust. Even if I must walk through this storm, I can do so with confidence. I know You will be with me. You not only calm the storm to a whisper; you whisper calm to my anxious heart. I am placing my life and welfare once again into Your hands, Lord.

DAILY TRUTH
The more you trust God, the more you'll trust God.

DAILY REFLECTIONS
Then we cried out, "Lord, help us! Rescue us!" And he did! God stilled the storm, calmed the waves, and he hushed the hurricane winds to only a whisper. We were so relieved, so glad as he guided us safely to harbor in a quiet haven. Psalm 107:28-30 TPT

When I felt my feet slipping, you came with your love and kept me steady. And when I was burdened with worries, you comforted me and made me feel secure. Psalm 94:18-19 CEV

"For the LORD your God is living among you. He is a mighty savior. He will take delight in you with gladness. With his love, he will calm all your fears. He will rejoice over you with joyful songs." Zephaniah 3:17 NLT

When you go through deep waters and great trouble, I will be with you. When you go through rivers of difficulty, you will not drown! Isaiah 43:2 TLB

DAILY CHALLENGE

What storms have made you afraid? How have you handled them? How has God calmed the turmoil in your life? What will you do the next time you feel a storm is brewing? Memorize Jesus' three words to the disciples in Mark 4:39 (KJV) and speak them out loud each time you need calm in your chaos.

DAILY THOUGHTS & PRAYERS

Day 56

When You're Longing for Home
The One Who Is Preparing a Place for You

*"There is more than enough room in my Father's home.
If this were not so, would I have told you
that I am going to prepare a place for you?
When everything is ready, I will come and get you,
so that you will always be with me where I am."*
John 14:2-3 NLT

FROM YOUR FAITHFUL FATHER'S HEART
My child, I understand the longing in your heart for heaven. I planted eternity in your heart. This imperfect and sinful world will never be your home. One day your time on earth will end. Your home on earth, as humble or spacious as it may be, will no longer concern you. I am preparing a new home where you will live one day along with all My children—all those who place their trust in Me. I am the Way, and I am the One who is preparing a place for you, but I will also come back to escort My children to heaven personally. I'm waiting for the perfect time when everything is ready. But until then, live in a state of readiness, not with dread for what may happen to you on earth, but with a hope-filled heart, eager to live in My presence forever. If I love you enough to give you an eternal dwelling place, could you not also prepare a welcome place for Me to live in your heart while you're earthbound?

FROM A GRATEFUL HEART
Lord, sometimes I ache to go home—to my real home with You. This earth and all of its problems are so temporary. Pain, suffering, trouble, frustration—all of these try to sneak under the covers as my constant companions. Yet You are the One who is preparing a place for me, a joy-full place in Your house for me. I can't wait to see my new room, Lord, and all my loved ones gone before me. But most of all, I'm looking forward to seeing

You. While I'm still earthbound, before You call me home, or before You return if we're still alive, I want You to always feel as welcome in my heart as You make me feel in Yours. Wherever You are, Lord, is where I want to live forever.

DAILY TRUTH
Home is in the joyful presence of the Lord.

DAILY REFLECTIONS
He has also planted eternity [a sense of divine purpose] in the human heart [a mysterious longing which nothing under the sun can satisfy, except God]—yet man cannot find out (comprehend, grasp) what God has done (His overall plan) from the beginning to the end. Ecclesiastes 3:11 AMP

"And you know the way where I am going." Thomas said to Him, "Lord, we do not know where You are going; how do we know the way?" Jesus said to him, "I am the way, and the truth, and the life; no one comes to the Father except through Me." John 14:4-6 NASB

"However, no one knows the day or hour when these things will happen, not even the angels in heaven or the Son himself. Only the Father knows." Matthew 24:36 NLT

And I pray that Christ will be more and more at home in your hearts, living within you as you trust in him. May your roots go down deep into the soil of God's marvelous love; and may you be able to feel and understand, as all God's children should, how long, how wide, how deep, and how high his love really is; and to experience this love for yourselves, though it is so great that you will never see the end of it or fully know or understand it. Ephesians 3:17-19 TLB

DAILY CHALLENGE

What are you anticipating the most about the new home Christ is preparing for you? How are we to prepare for His coming back to earth again? How are you preparing a place for Christ's presence in your heart while you live on earth? For further study on heaven and your final home, you might enjoy reading Randy Alcorn's book, *Heaven*.

DAILY THOUGHTS & PRAYERS

Day 57

When You Want to Give Up
The One Who Will Never Give Up On You

> *All God's gifts are right in front of you as you wait expectantly*
> *for our Master Jesus to arrive on the scene for the Finale.*
> *And not only that, but God himself is right alongside to keep you steady and*
> *on track until things are all wrapped up by Jesus. God, who got you started*
> *in this spiritual adventure, shares with us the life of his Son and our Master*
> *Jesus. He will never give up on you. Never forget that.*
> 1 Corinthians 1:7-9 MSG

FROM YOUR FAITHFUL FATHER'S HEART

My child, have your running shoes worn blisters on your feet? I know you are weary and want to give up at times. But I have not changed. I am the same faithful God who saw the world at its worst and destroyed all but one family—Noah's—because he believed and trusted in Me. And I am the same One who wants all to be saved. I have always been patient and long-suffering with people, sending them prophets and servants of Mine who would declare both My promises and My warnings. But I still work with all My children. Remember, I am the One who will never give up on you. I will give you the strength to keep running, to keep working, and to keep on trusting Me for all your needs until the day I call you home. I still long for your fellowship and will always be there for you. Never give up, child. Stay focused on Me. As long as people are lost, there is still work to do.

FROM A GRATEFUL HEART

Lord, You hear the deepest groans of my spirit when I feel like giving up. You listen to my complaints and love me anyway. Gently but firmly You prod me back into the race. Thank You for the ways You've always loved me and taught me. Whether through a teacher, through Your Word, through a difficulty or loss, or simply by Your Spirit's pressure on my heart, You have pursued me and continued to show me that You are the One who will never give up on me or any of Your children. You will never leave me. Lord, I desperately need Your continued strength and grace to keep moving ahead. When I'm tired and all I want to do is give up, You will provide the rest I need to press on. I am trusting You will be there to pick me up and nudge me forward. Thank You for never giving up on me. Help me to demonstrate Your love to others who are discouraged and tired so they can know who You really are and can experience Your strength and restoration.

DAILY TRUTH
God is the persistent Pursuer.

DAILY REFLECTIONS
"'From the time your ancestors left Egypt until now, day after day, again and again I sent you my servants the prophets.'" Jeremiah 7:25 NIV

"'You never waver in your covenant commitment, never give up on those who love you and do what you say.'" Daniel 9:4 MSG

The Lord is not slow in keeping his promise, as some understand slowness. Instead he is patient with you, not wanting anyone to perish, but everyone to come to repentance. 2 Peter 3:9 NIV

We are pressed on every side by troubles, but we are not crushed and broken. We are perplexed, because we don't know why things happen as they do, but we don't give up and quit. We are hunted down, but God never abandons us. We get knocked down, but we get up again and keep going. 2 Corinthians 4:8-9 TLB

DAILY CHALLENGE

Read the story of Noah in Genesis 6:8-8:22. Try to imagine what it would be like if you were Noah or one of his family members. Would you have kept believing God's faithfulness and persistence as long as Noah did? Why do you think God didn't give up on His creation and destroy even Noah and his family?

DAILY THOUGHTS & PRAYERS

Day 58

When Grief Overwhelms You
The One Who Is Acquainted with Grief

*He was despised and rejected—a man of sorrows,
acquainted with deepest grief.
We turned our backs on him and looked the other way.
He was despised, and we did not care.*
Isaiah 53:3 NLT

FROM YOUR FAITHFUL FATHER'S HEART
My child, you've been there, haven't you? Grief has sucked the life right out of you, leaving you a shell of your former self—at least for a time. Whether you lost a parent, a child, a spouse, or a friend, you can identify with those who have traveled the same path now, can't you? You may have even felt the sting of betrayal or disappointment. The One who is acquainted with grief knows and understands your pain. Only His grief has no comparison. My Son bore the sin penalty of the entire world. The former sin nature of all My children convicted them as if they were there, but Jesus offered forgiveness. When He wept, He wept for you. Remember, I sent My Holy Spirit to comfort you in times such as this. I see your tears. I hear your sighs. I understand your pain. Just be held today, My child. Rest in My arms. Because of My Son's sacrifice, all those who know and love Me will live with Me one day in heaven. Your grief will turn to joy.

FROM A GRATEFUL HEART
Lord, at times the grief in my soul is like a knife wound. It's almost too much to bear. The loss of a loved one leaves such a gaping hole in my heart that I struggle to even breathe. What will I do? How will I make it with this emptiness inside? But then I remember the grief You bore and the price You paid for my sin. You willingly gave Your life as a sacrifice for my wayward nature. And You refused to use Your power to halt the injustice. You suffered rejection, hate, and the deepest grief possible, because of the

outcome: the joy set before You, my salvation. I am the benefactor of Your grief and pain, though I helped cause it. I am the guilty one, yet You were the One punished. I am the one set free, all because You took my punishment and my death sentence. Thank You for Your comforting presence in times like this, Lord. For those who know and love You, death holds no power. One day, time and sorrow will be no more. Then, we will see our loved ones again, and You, face to face. Even in my deepest grief, I know You understand, Jesus. And I can go on because You paved the way. Hold me close, Lord. I need You so much!

DAILY TRUTH
Jesus' pain spelled our eternal gain.

DAILY REFLECTIONS
Jesus wept. John 11:35 KJV

For Jesus is not some high priest who has no sympathy for our weaknesses and flaws. He has already been tested in every way that we are tested; but He emerged victorious, without failing God. Hebrews 4:15 VOICE

He comforts us in all our troubles so that we can comfort others. When they are troubled, we will be able to give them the same comfort God has given us. 2 Corinthians 1:4 NLT

Looking unto Jesus the author and finisher of our faith; who for the joy that was set before him endured the cross, despising the shame, and is set down at the right hand of the throne of God. Hebrews 12:2 KJV

DAILY CHALLENGE
Review the times when you experienced grief. How did you get through them? Describe how God's comfort felt during those seasons. How have your times of grief and God's comfort made you more sensitive to others who go through similar situations?

DAILY THOUGHTS & PRAYERS

Day 59

When You're Walking Through the Fire
The One Who Is Able to Deliver You

> *"If we are thrown into the blazing furnace,*
> *the God we serve is able to deliver us from it,*
> *and he will deliver us from Your Majesty's hand.*
> *But even if he does not, we want you to know, Your Majesty,*
> *that we will not serve your gods*
> *or worship the image of gold you have set up."*
> Daniel 3:17-18 NIV

FROM YOUR FAITHFUL FATHER'S HEART

My child, are you confused by what you see in this life? Even My children experience tragedies. You watch the righteous fall with injustice, murder, or persecution. When you walk through your own fire, you can't explain what's happening. You wonder why bad things happen to good people. But I call committed followers who are willing to suffer for Me if necessary. I will help you live courageously. You can always count on My presence in the fire. I am the One who can deliver you just like I did Daniel's friends in the furnace. But if not, if I choose otherwise, I still want you to live and honor Me regardless of the cost—in life or death. My arms reach past the grave to bring you safely home when your purpose on earth is complete.

FROM A GRATEFUL HEART

Lord, I admit to being a wimpy Christian at times. I'm not sure if I can always say, "Thy will be done," when I'm walking through the fire. Yet I want to trust You in any situation: to love You so deeply and be so committed to You that my faith would soar at times like that. You can shut the mouth of lions. You can cool the fire in the furnace, and You can make a way to escape harm. You can do anything You desire because You are a sovereign God. But my heart wants to be so in tune with Yours that I can say, "But if not, Lord, if You choose to take me home instead, it's okay." I'm not afraid of suffering for You. I don't fear pain or the heat of flames. I will praise You in the fire. I just want what You want, Lord. More than anything, I want to honor You in life and death so that others can see—and know—the Jesus in me.

DAILY TRUTH
One life totally committed to Jesus is worth the cost—no matter what the price.

DAILY REFLECTIONS
So if you are suffering according to God's will, keep on doing what is right and trust yourself to the God who made you, for he will never fail you. 1 Peter 4:19 TLB

So I'm not defeated by my weakness, but delighted! For when I feel my weakness and endure mistreatment—when I'm surrounded with troubles on every side and face persecution because of my love for Christ—I am made yet stronger. For my weakness becomes a portal to God's power. 2 Corinthians 12:10 TPT

For to me to live is Christ, and to die is gain. Philippians 1:21 KJV

"When you walk through the fire of oppression, you will not be burned up; the flames will not consume you." Isaiah 43:2 NLT

DAILY CHALLENGE
Read the experience of Daniel's three friends in the fiery furnace in Daniel 3. Who was the fourth person in the fire? Read Daniel 1:1-20. Why do you think these young men could be so courageous and confident amid such terror? For further study, read about Daniel's experience in Daniel 6. Who did Daniel credit for this miracle?

DAILY THOUGHTS & PRAYERS

Day 60

When You Long for God's Grace and Goodness
The One Whose Kindness Leads Us to Repentance

Or do you despise the riches of His kindness, restraint, and patience, not recognizing that God's kindness is intended to lead you to repentance?
Romans 2:4 HCSB

FROM YOUR FAITHFUL FATHER'S HEART

My child, I have every right to exercise righteous anger. With one breath or one word, I can wipe out entire nations or send another flood and bury My world beneath a watery grave. I hold people accountable for their foolish choices and sinful ways. But I have given My faithful covenant never to destroy creation by flood again. My Son died to pay for those wrong choices. I want to bless you and all My children. I offer you hope and not despair. Because of My grace, I withhold My anger from those who refuse My love, because I want none to turn away. My consuming passion will always be drenched in My perfect goodness to seal you as My prisoner of love and draw you into close fellowship with Me. I am the One whose kindness led you to repentance, and I offer My goodness to all.

FROM A GRATEFUL HEART

Lord, even the people You loved turned against You in Bible times and worshipped other gods. Your creation chose rules rather than embracing a relationship with Your precious Son. Our sinful choices cut You like a sharp knife after all the miraculous things You had done. Yet knowing we could never overcome sin on our own, You sent Jesus to die for us—for me. You poured out all Your righteous anger upon Him so Your love would cover me. Your gracious forgiveness and faithful love ignite a fresh flame in my heart for You. I will always long for Your continued grace and goodness, Lord. One day all mankind will stand before You in judgment. But as long as we have breath, You are the One whose kindness and undeserved grace leads all of us to repentance.

DAILY TRUTH
Perfect love drives out fear and creates a consuming passion for God.

DAILY REFLECTIONS
"Whenever I bring clouds over the earth and the rainbow appears in the clouds, I will remember my covenant between me and you and all living creatures of every kind. Never again will the waters become a flood to destroy all life." Genesis 9:14-15 NIV

But our ancestors acted arrogantly; they became stiff-necked and did not listen to Your commands. They refused to listen and did not remember Your wonders You performed among them. They became stiff-necked and appointed a leader to return to their slavery in Egypt. But You are a forgiving God, gracious and compassionate, slow to anger and rich in faithful love, and You did not abandon them. Nehemiah 9:16-17 HCBS

So all of you, watch yourselves! Don't forget the covenant that the LORD your God made with you by making an idol or an image of any kind or anything the LORD your God forbids, because the LORD your God is an all-consuming fire. He is a passionate God. Deuteronomy 4:23-24 CEB

Fasten me upon your heart as a seal of fire forevermore. This living, consuming flame will seal you as my prisoner of love. My passion is stronger than the chains of death and the grave, all consuming as the very flashes of fire from the burning heart of God. Place this fierce, unrelenting fire over your entire being. Song of Solomon 8:6 TPT

DAILY CHALLENGE
Read Deuteronomy 4:32-40. What were some of the ways God showed His goodness to His people? What are some ways you have experienced His grace and goodness? How did God's kindness lead you to repentance? Why is He so passionate about His love for people? How does sin grieve God's heart? How does it grieve yours? What can you do about it?

DAILY THOUGHTS & PRAYERS

Day 61

When You Long for Godly Leaders
The One Who Is Lord of Kings

Then King Nebuchadnezzar fell prostrate before Daniel and paid him honor and ordered that an offering and incense be presented to him. The king said to Daniel, "Surely your God is the God of gods and the Lord of kings."
Daniel 2:46-47 NIV

FROM YOUR FAITHFUL FATHER'S HEART
My child, no king rises to power on his own. No ruler or authority exercises lordship over people without My allowance. I am the One who is Lord of earthly kings. Throughout history, I have used heathen nations and kings to discipline My people who turned to other gods. But no one can match My majesty and power. Don't fret over ungodly leaders. Pray for them. Remember I long for everyone to trust and acknowledge Me, and I can turn the hearts of kings and authorities according to My will. While wicked rulers may lead for a time, they will eventually fall. I offer every person a choice, including presidents, prime ministers, and rulers around the world. But when they ignore Me and refuse to follow Me as the one true God, they are sealing their fate. Pray for your leaders to acknowledge Me and to look to Me for wisdom. My miraculous works and power, when seen through spiritual eyes, bring the right confession: "He is Lord over all kings; He is Lord indeed!"

FROM A GRATEFUL HEART
Lord, I pray for the day when every person in authority will look to You for righteous living and godly leadership. I've heard about nations that fell and rulers who suffered because of foolish actions. Even current leaders often fail to connect the dots that lead to Your faithful hand. But those who choose not to follow You as Lord will painfully miss out on Your divine plan and fellowship. On the other hand, what a blessing to see how You

turn the hearts of rulers when their eyes are opened and they recognize Your power. And how blessed is the nation who acknowledges You as Lord! For a season, ungodly leaders may appear to escape as they wreak havoc wherever they go. But one day every knee will bow and every tongue will confess that Jesus is Lord—even the very ones who refused to believe. I long for righteous leaders, and I purpose to pray for them. But I also trust that even when ungodly authority figures rule, they must give an account to You. You are the One—and only One—who is Lord of kings.

DAILY TRUTH
God is the only One who can change a heart to acknowledge Him.

DAILY REFLECTIONS
Blessed is the nation whose God is the Lord; and the people whom he hath chosen for his own inheritance. Psalm 33:12 KJV

For in due season Christ will be revealed from heaven by the blessed and only Almighty God, the King of kings and Lord of lords, who alone can never die, who lives in light so terrible that no human being can approach him. No mere man has ever seen him nor ever will. Unto him be honor and everlasting power and dominion forever and ever. Amen. 1 Timothy 6:15-16 TLB

Be still before the Lord and wait patiently for him; do not fret when people succeed in their ways, when they carry out their wicked schemes. Psalm 37:7 NIV

The king's heart is in the hand of the Lord, Like the rivers of water; He turns it wherever He wishes. Proverbs 21:1 NKJV

DAILY CHALLENGE

Take five minutes a day to pray for those in high leadership positions wherever you live. Pray for presidents, prime ministers, kings, and other government officials. Use 1 Timothy 2:1-3 as a guide. Memorize 2 Chronicles 7:14, and pray for a time of confession, repentance, and healing in your land.

DAILY THOUGHTS & PRAYERS

Day 62

When You Need Divine Intervention
The One Who Intervenes for You

These amazing things had never been heard of before;
you did things never dreamed of!
No one perceived your greatness.
No eye has ever seen a God like you,
who intervenes for those who wait and long for you!
Isaiah 64:4 TPT

FROM YOUR FAITHFUL FATHER'S HEART
My child, no conceivable god, whether built of wood, plastic, gold, or steel, could ever compare to Me. For I am the one, true, Almighty God. Around the world, people worship idols of their own making, and they end up mirroring their own gods. Their lives stagnate, ending in futility. But I will always be the One who intervenes for you and those who wait and long for Me. Those who worship Me with their whole heart, soul, and mind will find unimaginable joys in an intimate relationship with Me. I see your heart and love to act on behalf of the ones who fear Me and place their hope in Me. As you study My Word, you'll see My miraculous acts and amazing deeds. In those pages, you will find My love letter written for you and for all who desire to truly know Me. And you'll understand why no god will ever compare to My compassion, grace, and intervention. You will never find one who loves you as I do.

FROM A GRATEFUL HEART
Lord, everything in my life needs Your divine intervention. I couldn't function without You. From finances to relationships, to wisdom and salvation, nothing will work without You. Is there anything You won't do for those who love You and seek to honor You? Though others have tried to thwart Your purposes, corrupt Your name, and even deny Your existence, boasting of their successes, they can only experience Your power and miracles by

acknowledging You and believing in You. You are the One who intervenes for those who continually wait on You, with You, and for You. When this world has taken its last breath, no one will ever deny You again. Your name and Your actions will live on in those who will worship You forever. Thank You for allowing me to know You and to be part of that immense congregation one day in eternity. I am so blessed because of the ways You have intervened in my life.

DAILY TRUTH
God transforms our good works into God-works when we honor Him.

DAILY REFLECTIONS
The idols of the nations are merely things of silver and gold, shaped by human hands. They have mouths but cannot speak, and eyes but cannot see. They have ears but cannot hear, and mouths but cannot breathe. And those who make idols are just like them, as are all who trust in them. Psalm 135:15-18 NLT

Great are the works of the Lord; they are pondered by all who delight in them. Psalm 111:2 NIV

I write this to you whose experience with God is as life-changing as ours, all due to our God's straight dealing and the intervention of our God and Savior, Jesus Christ. Grace and peace to you many times over as you deepen in your experience with God and Jesus, our Master. 2 Peter 1:1-2 MSG

God, King of Israel, your Redeemer, God-of-the-Angel-Armies, says: "I'm first, I'm last, and everything in between. I'm the only God there is. Who compares with me?" Isaiah 44:6 MSG

DAILY CHALLENGE

When has God intervened in your life? In your family? At work? Where else have you seen His divine intervention in the lives of other believers? Record some of those experiences and review them often.

DAILY THOUGHTS & PRAYERS

Day 63

When Things Are Hard to Understand
The One Whose Thoughts Are Not Your Thoughts

"My thoughts are nothing like your thoughts," says the Lord.
"And my ways are far beyond anything you could imagine.
For just as the heavens are higher than the earth,
so my ways are higher than your ways
and my thoughts higher than your thoughts."
Isaiah 55:8-9 NLT

FROM YOUR FAITHFUL FATHER'S HEART

My child, look at the heavens and the sun, moon, and stars. How high do those hang from the earth? My thoughts are like that. They are different than yours, higher than your thoughts. Your pattern of thinking is earthbound. I give My children discernment, but there are spiritual realms you can't possibly see right now. I'm working behind the scenes in ways unknown to you. You can never push beyond the finiteness of your brain until I give you an eternal, glorified body. So why do you try to figure things out by yourself, instead of trusting Me? Read My Word. I've promised to direct your paths, to guide you daily, and to give you wisdom. But some things will never unfold until I make them clear one day. Right now, you see Me as if looking through a blurry mirror, unable to visualize the future except by faith. One day, all that will change, and you will see Me face to face and understand things clearly. I am the One whose thoughts are not your thoughts. But you are always safe in My hands.

FROM A GRATEFUL HEART

Lord, so many times I've pleaded and prodded (and ranted and raved) trying to persuade You to see my way of thinking. As if I knew better. I am not God. And You are the One whose thoughts are not my thoughts. Your otherworldliness comforts me at times, but then it leaves me trembling on other occasions. Yet my heart longs to completely release my faulty reasoning and embrace the faith You've already given me. I confess trying to accomplish or understand things on my own at times, and neglecting to search Your Word for needed wisdom. I do trust You, Lord. Your plans are always best, and Your ways are perfect. I look forward to the day when everything will unfold, and I'll finally understand what I can't possibly comprehend now.

DAILY TRUTH
God's thoughts never waver. Neither do His promises.

DAILY REFLECTIONS
The LORD says, "I will guide you along the best pathway for your life. I will advise you and watch over you." Psalm 32:8 NLT

In the same way, we can see and understand only a little about God now, as if we were peering at his reflection in a poor mirror; but someday we are going to see him in his completeness, face-to-face. Now all that I know is hazy and blurred, but then I will see everything clearly, just as clearly as God sees into my heart right now. 1 Corinthians 13:12 TLB

Because of our faith, Christ has brought us into this place of undeserved privilege where we now stand, and we confidently and joyfully look forward to sharing God's glory. Romans 5:2 NLT

It will all happen in a moment, in the twinkling of an eye, when the last trumpet is blown. For there will be a trumpet blast from the sky, and all the Christians who have died will suddenly become alive, with new bodies that will never, never die; and then we who are still alive shall suddenly have new bodies too. 1 Corinthians 15:52 TLB

DAILY CHALLENGE

What happened the last time you tried to assemble something without the instruction manual? How difficult was that experience? When was the last time you tried to solve a deeper problem on your own? How did that work out? What would your life be like if you were in control, not God? Thank your faithful Father today that His ways are not your ways and His thoughts are not your thoughts.

DAILY THOUGHTS & PRAYERS

Day 64

When You Need God's Protective Covering
The One Who Covers You with His Shadow

*Have mercy on me, O God, have mercy!
I look to you for protection. I will hide beneath the shadow
of your wings until the danger passes by.*
Psalm 57:1 NLT

FROM YOUR FAITHFUL FATHER'S HEART
My child, My plans will always trump yours. I watch the big picture at all times, working constantly to complete the drama I first began. You are such a small part of that play, yet you are on mission for Me. I have given you My Word, and I love you so much. Stay close to Me, because I constantly hide you and all My children from those who want to harm or destroy you. I am powerful enough that even the mere shadow of My protection brings the covering you need for safety. I am the same One who created the heavens and the earth, who parted the Red Sea, and who sets the prisoner free. And I am the faithful One who writes His promises on your heart and declares that you belong to Me. Even when clouds try to obscure your path, remember that those shadows are under My control. I am the One who covers you with the shadow of My wings, and to live under My shadow is to live in My Spirit's presence. I visualize the best in you and work to bring that good to fruition. All My plans for you—and this world—will one day be completed, when Jesus returns. Those who belong to Me will not be left behind.

FROM A GRATEFUL HEART
Lord, I love living under Your shelter, in Your presence, and making my home in the place where Your shadow covers me. I confess my foolishness at moving out from under Your umbrella of protection at times. I've felt the attacks of my enemy when I left Your safety. Those painful lessons remind me that I need You constantly. You are not deaf; You hear my cries for help and bring me back. Lord, until the day You call me home, I want to

keep Your Word on my lips and my confidence in Your faithfulness. Help me share the good news about You with those around me. No one can thwart Your eternal purposes. You are still the One who covers me with Your shadow. The shade of Your protection reaches far enough to protect all Your children from the heat of the enemy. And You never move away.

DAILY TRUTH
If the shadow of God's wings offers such symbolic protection, imagine what Almighty God Himself is like.

DAILY REFLECTIONS
Whoever dwells in the shelter of the Most High will rest in the shadow of the Almighty. Psalm 91:1 NIV

Listen! The LORD's arm is not too weak to save you, nor is his ear too deaf to hear you call. Isaiah 59:1 NLT

Give thanks to him who parted the Red Sea. His faithful love endures forever. Psalm 136:13 NLT

We can make our plans, but the final outcome is in God's hands. Proverbs 16:1 TLB

DAILY CHALLENGE
Read Psalm 91, and consider memorizing it. Although this chapter may be interpreted as a Messianic psalm, its message can be applied to your life. List the applicable truths and principles you find in this chapter. Thank God that His shadow, the spirit of His presence, covers you, night and day.

DAILY THOUGHTS & PRAYERS

Day 65

When You Long to See God's Miracles
The One Who Demonstrates His Holy Power

*The LORD has demonstrated his holy power
before the eyes of all the nations.
All the ends of the earth will see the victory of our God.*
Isaiah 52:10 NLT

FROM YOUR FAITHFUL FATHER'S HEART
My child, through the centuries nations have watched and witnessed My deliverance of captives, the healing of the sick, and the raising of the dead. My Son brought My message to the world, the message of victory to every person: forgiveness, peace, and reconciliation to a holy God. And through Jesus, every person who believes will one day see—and know—that I am truly the One who demonstrates His holy power. But maybe it's been a while since you've recognized My power at work. You feel weak, and you long to experience My miraculous hand on your life again. Be encouraged today. Sometimes miracles hide until you open your faith eyes wide. I still move mountains; I still work miracles; and I still change hearts and lives today, just as I've done through the ages. Don't be afraid to ask, My child. I am Almighty God, the One who demonstrates My holy power, the kind that shows I am undoubtedly the only God. Who else would care enough to heal the holes in your heart that you cannot fix yourself? Who else would drape you with a righteous robe and declare that you are My Beloved? Keep believing, My child.

FROM A GRATEFUL HEART
Lord, when difficult situations press in, and all I can see is confusion around me, I long to see Your miracles and Your power at work. My needs are like giants. They overpower me at times, trying to shatter my faith. I still believe, but help my unbelief. Sometimes I look at my circumstances instead of Your Word, Your promises, and Your track record of faithfulness. But

You are teaching me that miracles appear every day: a baby's newborn cry, a garden filled with flowers, Your fresh morning mercies, and a life reborn by Your Spirit. You demonstrated Your power ultimately by winning over death through Jesus' perfect sacrifice on the cross. Though I am weak, I choose to trust in You, Your strength, and Your power. Thank You, Lord, that You are the One who demonstrates His holy power daily.

DAILY TRUTH
God's miraculous power not only demonstrates His divine love; it completely covers our sinfulness.

DAILY REFLECTIONS
"The Spirit of the Lord is on me, because he has anointed me to proclaim good news to the poor. He has sent me to proclaim freedom for the prisoners and recovery of sight for the blind, to set the oppressed free, to proclaim the year of the Lord's favor." Luke 4:18-19 NIV

God made him who had no sin to be sin for us, so that in him we might become the righteousness of God. 2 Corinthians 5:21 NIV

"Lord, the God of our ancestors, are you not the God who is in heaven? You rule over all the kingdoms of the nations. Power and might are in your hand, and no one can withstand you." 2 Chronicles 20:6 NIV

O Lord, our God, no one can compare with you. Such wonderful works and miracles are all found with you! And you think of us all the time with your countless expressions of love—far exceeding our expectations! Psalm 40:5 TPT

DAILY CHALLENGE

Take a moment to list all the big and small miracles you have seen or experienced in your lifetime. Are there any hidden miracles you have not recognized until now? How have you seen God's power work in your own life? In the lives of others? What miracle do you need in your life right now?

DAILY THOUGHTS & PRAYERS

Day 66

When You Need to Remember Sin's Magnitude
The One Who Took Your Punishment

But it was our sins that did that to him,
that ripped and tore and crushed him—our sins!
He took the punishment, and that made us whole.
Through his bruises we get healed.
Isaiah 53:5 MSG

FROM YOUR FAITHFUL FATHER'S HEART
My child, never call sin insignificant—something you can toss aside like the leftovers of an ordinary meal. The moment sin becomes ordinary, you've misplaced—and misunderstood—the impact of your sinful nature. I am the One who took your punishment. Sin corrupted every person and left them terminally ill apart from My intervention. And yet, look at My solution. I freed you and was crushed for your sins. On the day I was crucified, I took upon Myself every ugly sin ever committed. And, in earthly flesh, I received your chastisement that day so you could be healed. Can you ever forget the humiliation I experienced, the beatings I received, the nails I bore, and the unreal price I paid so you wouldn't have to endure that kind of penalty? In this life, you will experience a measure of suffering, but not the forever kind of separation that would have sealed your fate forever, had I not stepped in. Then I rose again, destroying death's sting forever! The magnitude of your sin was great. But always remember: My grace was greater.

FROM A GRATEFUL HEART
Lord, where do I begin to thank You? You are the One who took my punishment! I'm the one who deserved to die. Words can never express what I feel. I can never fully repay the debt for my sin. Yet You don't require payment from me. May I never forget the magnitude of my sin and the price of what You did for me, and what You do every day of my life. You forgave me.

You released me from eternal imprisonment. You filled my heart with joy and You are giving me a full, abundant life. You gave me Your Holy Spirit to live in my heart daily. I am so grateful that the troubles and pressures of this life can never diminish Your love for me. My enemies have no power to steal or destroy my relationship with You. What amazing grace! You bless me and You are leading me on the path and in the plan You have designed for me. I will eternally thank You.

DAILY TRUTH

You won't understand the magnitude of God's grace until you realize the magnitude of your own sin.

DAILY REFLECTIONS

All have turned away, all have become corrupt; there is no one who does good, not even one. Psalm 14:3 NIV

We—every one of us—have strayed away like sheep! We, who left God's paths to follow our own. Yet God laid on him the guilt and sins of every one of us! Isaiah 53:6 TLB

Who could ever divorce us from the endless love of God's Anointed One? Absolutely no one! For nothing in the universe has the power to diminish his love toward us. Troubles, pressures, and problems are unable to come between us and heaven's love. What about persecutions, deprivations, dangers, and death threats? No, for they are all impotent to hinder omnipotent love. Romans 8:35 TPT

He was sheer weakness and humiliation when he was killed on the cross, but oh, he's alive now—in the mighty power of God! 2 Corinthians 13:4 MSG

DAILY CHALLENGE

If you know the words to a song that describes Jesus' death on the cross for you, either an old hymn or a current praise song, sing those words out loud. Or look up a song on the internet about Jesus' death, and read through the lyrics, or listen to it, focusing on the words. Write a personal letter to Jesus, thanking Him for taking your punishment upon Himself. Include how His forgiveness has changed and healed you.

DAILY THOUGHTS & PRAYERS

Day 67

When You're Feeling Forgotten
The One Who Will Never Forget You

*"Can a mother forget the infant at her breast,
walk away from the baby she bore?
But even if mothers forget, I'd never forget you—never.
Look, I've written your names on the backs of my hands."*
Isaiah 49:15-16 MSG

FROM YOUR FAITHFUL FATHER'S HEART
My child, sometimes you fail to remember your true identity. I made you, forming you with My own hands. And I have given every person I created the opportunity to reclaim that forgetfulness, that rebellion that began with Adam and Eve. I long to bless you and all My creation and to draw you into deeper fellowship with Me. If you will follow Me, I will lead you and give you wisdom for each day. The choice is yours. I am the One who will never forget you, even though you may temporarily forget your roots. I remember you, but I forget your sins. I no longer hold them to your account. When you become My child by faith, you belong to Me forever. And My perfect memory will always remember you and guard that relationship. You are much more precious to Me than an earthly babe to its mother. I never forget who and whose My children are.

FROM A GRATEFUL HEART
Lord, I'm so brain-challenged at times, forgetting the most important things in life: family, friends, and even You, Lord. I confess the times my memory has taken a vacation, darting from one interest to another, always searching for the most meaningful path, the most adventurous ride, or the most comfortable lifestyle. I try to recall Your promises, but they remain hidden, especially when I fail to tuck them into my heart. You are my purpose, Lord. You are my joy. You are my God—the One who will never forget me. When I stop and remember that I belong to You and that Your

faithfulness is unquestionable, I can refocus. Lord, may I never forget You, Your Word, what You've done for me, and all You've promised for eternity!

DAILY TRUTH
The names of God's children are permanently etched on His hands with the blood of Christ.

DAILY REFLECTIONS
You made me; you created me. Now give me the sense to follow your commands. Psalm 119:73 NLT

Everyone dies because all of us are related to Adam, being members of his sinful race, and wherever there is sin, death results. But all who are related to Christ will rise again. 1 Corinthians 15:22 TLB

"I, even I, am he who blots out your transgressions, for my own sake, and remembers your sins no more." Isaiah 43:25 NIV

He remembered us in our weakness. His faithful love endures forever. Psalm 136:23 NLT

DAILY CHALLENGE
God's animal creatures and human moms possess fierce loyalty and love for their babies. Although you may hear of children left accidentally in a hot car, those experiences are not common. What comparison does God draw in Isaiah 49:15-16 regarding mothers? How does God's perfect memory make you feel? What things do you most forget? This week, tie a string around your finger just to remind you that God never forgets you—and as a reminder for you to seek Him daily.

DAILY THOUGHTS & PRAYERS

Day 68

When You're Searching for Truth
The One Who Exposes Lies

*"I expose the false prophets as liars
and make fools of fortune-tellers."*
Isaiah 44:25 NLT

FROM YOUR FAITHFUL FATHER'S HEART
My child, do you have trouble discerning the truth? Since ancient times, false prophets have twisted My truth, even under oath, trying to deceive My children. But their words ring hollow and will always fail. They are like fortune-tellers, whose eyes and hearts are closed and darkened. These puffy clouds of pride never deliver truth. They predict times and seasons without knowledge, and they speak lies even to My children. But listen to My words. I am the One who exposes lies. Your persistent enemy wants to destroy you by whispering lies and half-truths to deceive you. His reasoning may sound good, but it leads to heartache and heartbreak. But I am relentless in My love for you. When you know the Truth, you will recognize those lies. My Word is the Truth you need, and through My Holy Spirit of Truth who lives in you, I will help you to be wise, to discern evil, and to act confidently on My promises. Whatever I say, you can believe. I will never lead you astray. I can never and will never be unfaithful to you or My Word.

FROM A GRATEFUL HEART
Lord, through the years many have tried to dictate Your actions, steal Your power, or deceive Your children, insisting they are the correct interpreters of truth. They dream up designs for the future and then scheme for success. And I've fallen for a few of their lies. But Lord, time and time again, their words rise like hot-air balloons, drifting aimlessly. We need Your truth in our world today, Lord. So many are calling wrong, right, and right, wrong. Even those in authority try to twist the truth and make laws to replace what You have declared since the beginning of time. And because of modern

technology, inaccurate stories spread like fire across our world, persuading the foolish to believe without questioning. Only You provide the right answers. You are the One who exposes lies and false prophets. You puncture their balloons with needle-sharp accuracy. Thank You for giving me Your Word so I can study and accurately discern what's right. Thank You for Your Spirit, who leads me into all truth and uncovers every lie. And thank You for being the Way, the Truth, and the Life.

DAILY TRUTH
God is a truth-teller, not a fortune-teller.

DAILY REFLECTIONS
Save me! Rescue me from the power of my enemies. Their mouths are full of lies; they swear to tell the truth, but they lie instead. Psalm 144:11 NLT

Truthful words stand the test of time, but lies are soon exposed. Proverbs 12:19 NLT

"And I will ask the Father and he will give you another Savior, the Holy Spirit of Truth, who will be to you a friend just like me—and he will never leave you. The world won't receive him because they can't see him or know him. But you will know him intimately, because he will make his home in you and will live inside you." John 14:16-17 TPT

If we are not faithful, he will still be faithful, because he must be true to who he is. 2 Timothy 2:13 ICB

DAILY CHALLENGE
Have you ever believed a lie or told one? What happened when the truth was revealed? Where do you go to find the truth about something? How has God's Word spoken truth to you? List some of those things that you believe about God and His Word. What will you do to make sure you are hearing the truth about a situation?

DAILY THOUGHTS & PRAYERS

Day 69

When You're Feeling Anxious and Distressed
The One Who Is Your Only Rock

*He alone is my rock and my salvation,
my fortress where I will never be shaken.*
Psalm 62:2 NLT

FROM YOUR FAITHFUL FATHER'S HEART
My child, who do you consult in times of trouble, pain, or distress? Where do you turn? Am I your first thought or your last? I alone am the One who is your rock and salvation. You can run to Me for your shelter, for I am unshakeable. I alone deserve your complete and undivided trust. My name and My character are rock solid and impenetrable. No dynamite can explode them; no earthquake can destroy them; no power can move them. No one can touch you when I am defending you. No matter what happens, you can remain firm, unshaken, and immoveable, because I will place you behind the rock of My name and character. Without Me, your life will be exposed, laid bare to enemies of fear, doubt, and unrest. I am not only your Rock, I am your *only* Rock and safe place of shelter.

FROM A GRATEFUL HEART
Lord, when I think of all the times I've run for a shallow cover or hidden behind pebbles or sandbags stacked hastily for protection, I feel so foolish. No fleshly efforts will ward off the destruction or temptation that waits to trip me up. I need something—someone—stronger than my weak defenses. You are that Rock, Lord. You are my only shelter, the One who is my only Rock. You've promised that when I'm stressed and burdens are trying to weigh me down, I can come to You. You will give me sweet rest. Help me to recognize the stressful trials as tools for You to shape me and rearrange me. Through those difficult times, You will teach me patience, enlarge my faith, and help me see things I couldn't visualize earlier—if I will only let You. A minefield of traps lay buried daily, waiting to destroy me. But You

have cleared the path. When I'm clueless as to what to do, Lord, I want to turn to You first, not last. You fill me with confidence, not in myself, but in a God who waits to protect and defend His children. In You, I am unshakeable. My knees don't quiver in fear. My heart is at rest, because You rescue me, Lord. You are my only Rock and my only place of true safety.[1]

DAILY TRUTH
The Rock of Ages is still the Rock of all ages.

DAILY REFLECTIONS
"There is no one holy like the LORD; there is no one besides you; there is no Rock like our God." 1 Samuel 2:2 NIV

But as for me, I will sing of Your strength; Yes, I will joyfully sing of Your faithfulness in the morning, For You have been my refuge, And a place of refuge on the day of my distress. Psalm 59:16 NASB

"Yes, trust in the Lord Yahweh forever and ever! For Yah, the Lord God, is your Rock of Ages!" Isaiah 26:4 TPT

From the ends of the earth I call to you, I call as my heart grows faint; lead me to the rock that is higher than I. Psalm 61:2 NIV

DAILY CHALLENGE
Search other Bible verses about the Rock. Why do you think this image is used repeatedly about God? To remind you that God is your unshakeable Rock, do one of two things: (1) Place a small rock on a bedside table or near a workspace. (2) If you have a garden, find or buy a large rock and put it in your garden in a prominent place.

DAILY THOUGHTS & PRAYERS

Day 70

When You Don't Understand God's Mercy
The One Who Is Rich in Mercy

*But God is so rich in mercy, and he loved us so much,
that even though we were dead because of our sins,
he gave us life when he raised Christ from the dead.
(It is only by God's grace that you have been saved!)*
Ephesians 2:4-5 NLT

FROM YOUR FAITHFUL FATHER'S HEART
My child, nothing you can say or do will ever change My love for you. I could have rejected you because of the sin that separates Me from all My creation. Once sin entered the world, it was as if My fellowship with man died. Nothing has been the same since. But I loved you too much to leave you alone. I wove the deadness of your sins into the grave clothes I wore. But then I rose again. I am not stingy with My mercy. Picture yourself in a coffin. Then visualize that lid flung open, and you are set free, with another chance at true, purposeful living. That's My mercy and grace at work. You could have remained dead in your sin. But the moment you accepted My payment to cover your penalty and chose to receive My mercy, you became truly alive. I am the One who is rich in mercy. I love you so much, My child. You were worth saving.

FROM A GRATEFUL HEART
Lord, I know what it's like to feel "dead," emotionally and spiritually separated from You. And I would not choose that existence, if you call it an existence, ever again. I love life too much. You are the One who is rich in mercy, the One who loved me even when I was living like a dead person—oblivious to Your goodness and true life. Thank You for Your mercy, for not giving me what I deserved. Thank You for making a way for me through Your death so that I could experience Your rich salvation and grace. You didn't reject me; You accepted me. You released me from death but buried

my old "grave clothes" in the coffin of my past. Because of Your limitless mercy and faithfulness, I can see, feel, hear, and celebrate new life with You daily.

DAILY TRUTH
Mercy is God's way of saying, "I paid it all."

DAILY REFLECTIONS
So it is God who decides to show mercy. We can neither choose it nor work for it. Romans 9:16 NLT

But God had mercy on me so that Christ Jesus could use me as a prime example of his great patience with even the worst sinners. Then others will realize that they, too, can believe in him and receive eternal life. 1 Timothy 1:16 NLT

Now Christ lives his life in you! And even though your body may be dead because of the effects of sin, his life-giving Spirit imparts life to you because you are fully accepted by God. Romans 8:10 TPT

But you, O Lord, your mercy-seat love is limitless, reaching higher than the highest heavens. Your great faithfulness is infinite, stretching over the whole earth. Psalm 36:5 TPT

DAILY CHALLENGE
When you think about the meaning of mercy in a court of law, how would you define it? How does that compare to God's mercy? Why is God's mercy greater? Look up the words to the old hymn, "Jesus Paid It All" (or quote by memory). What do those words mean to you?

DAILY THOUGHTS & PRAYERS

Day 71

When Life Is a Confusing Mystery
The One Who Reveals Mysteries

"But there is a God in heaven who reveals mysteries."
Daniel 2:28 HCSB

FROM YOUR FAITHFUL FATHER'S HEART
My child, are you troubled by things that are hidden from you, mysteries known only in heaven? I am not the author of confusion. Even though you may long to see the whole picture, you can never understand completely My activity in this world. I am the only One who knows the future. However, I will reveal some mysteries to My children. Listen carefully each day. As My child, you can discern My voice. Learn to trust Me. The thoughts I give to you will always agree with My words in the Bible. Never twist My words. The entire gospel has been revealed from beginning to end. I am the One who reveals mysteries that are discernible to My children. I am the Author of love, joy, and peace. If you keep My words close to your heart, they will give you wisdom and help just when you need them most.

FROM A GRATEFUL HEART
Lord, You are revealing Yourself in countries all over the world, drawing people to Yourself through dreams and visions. You speak through the Bible, through Your Spirit, through creation, and so many other ways. Your love for people makes You a God who passionately pursues the lost. But there are so many mysteries that still seem hidden to me, Lord. At times, the whys and hows of life confuse me. That's when it's hardest for me to fully understand. But in those sweet, precious times, both in the darkness and the light, when You have whispered Your truths to me—those revealed in Your Word—I find the strength to continue. In those "aha" moments, You give me the courage and motivation to continue on this journey. Thank You for being the One who reveals mysteries. Teach me when to share the deep things You reveal—and when to simply treasure them in my heart.

One day, we will understand completely all You want us to know. I look forward to that day in heaven, Lord.

DAILY TRUTH
More trust, less confusion.

DAILY REFLECTIONS
Yes, if you want better insight and discernment, and are searching for them as you would for lost money or hidden treasure, then wisdom will be given you and knowledge of God himself; you will soon learn the importance of reverence for the Lord and of trusting him. Proverbs 2:3-5 TLB

"I will pour out my Spirit upon all people. Your sons and daughters will prophesy. Your old men will dream dreams, and your young men will see visions." Joel 2:28 NLT

Every word of God proves true. He defends all who come to him for protection. Do not add to his words, lest he rebuke you, and you be found a liar. Proverbs 30:5-6 TLB

"Only I can tell you the future before it even happens. Everything I plan will come to pass, for I do whatever I wish." Isaiah 46:10 NLT

DAILY CHALLENGE
Ask the Lord to reveal Himself to you this week. As you study the Bible, look at the context of each passage and who is speaking or writing. Ask God, "How can I apply these words to my life?" Underline any "aha" truths that are especially meaningful to you, and record any verses you would like to memorize or study further.

DAILY THOUGHTS & PRAYERS

Day 72

When You Fear Not Having Enough
The One Who Became Poor to Make You Rich

You know how full of love and kindness our Lord Jesus was: though he was so very rich, yet to help you he became so very poor, so that by being poor he could make you rich.
2 Corinthians 8:9 TLB

FROM YOUR FAITHFUL FATHER'S HEART
My child, how often have I reminded you of My love for you? All the wealth of heaven is Mine. Yet I chose to step down and live a pauper's life, from birth to death. Why? So you could know what "rich" really means. I am the One who became poor to make you rich. Following Me does not guarantee you mansions on earth or millions in the bank. But because of what I did for you, you received an inheritance that is real. You may even be poor in material wealth, but you are wealthy in the things that matter. Gold can't buy you happiness or peace. Earthly possessions won't follow you to heaven. But the forgiveness, joy, and love I give you will last forever. Not only that, I will bless you with enough resources so that you can minister to others who have both physical and spiritual needs. You can become My hands on earth to help others. If you love Me, you will always have enough, My child.

FROM A GRATEFUL HEART
Lord, forgive my foolish complaints and misplaced desires. Even when I've felt "financially challenged," You have been so faithful to me. You have given me everything I could ever want or need. I want to be a channel of blessing to others, ready to give out of poverty or wealth. It all belongs to You, Lord. If I cling to the blessings You give me, they will shrivel and decay like leftover manna. You are the One who became poor to make me rich. I can never give You—or others—enough. Enlarge my love quotient, Lord. Help me to share the rich wealth of goodness, patience, and kindness that You

have entrusted to me. If all I have is You, Lord, that is enough!

DAILY TRUTH
God requires believing, not begging.

DAILY REFLECTIONS
Day by day the Lord takes care of the innocent, and they will receive an inheritance that lasts forever. They will not be disgraced in hard times; even in famine they will have more than enough. Psalm 37:18-19 NLT

He who loves money shall never have enough. The foolishness of thinking that wealth brings happiness! Ecclesiastes 5:10 TLB

And God will generously provide all you need. Then you will always have everything you need and plenty left over to share with others. 2 Corinthians 9:8 NLT

For he has conquered us with his great love, and his kindness has melted our hearts. His faithfulness lasts forever and he will never fail you. Psalm 117:2 TPT

DAILY CHALLENGE
When money is tight, how do you respond? Ask God to use your resources to help meet the physical needs of others who are hurting. If necessary, give up something you enjoy and donate that money to a worthy organization or someone in need. Read about God's provision of manna in Exodus 16:1-31. What happened when people failed to trust God for His daily manna? What lesson can we learn about God's faithfulness from their experience?

DAILY THOUGHTS & PRAYERS

Day 73

When You Need a Warrior
The One Who Is the Mighty Warrior

"The Lord your God is with you, the Mighty Warrior who saves. He will take great delight in you; in his love he will no longer rebuke you, but will rejoice over you with singing."
Zephaniah 3:17 NIV

FROM YOUR FAITHFUL FATHER'S HEART
My child, you are so important to Me. I called you so you could make My name known to those who don't know Me and to those who refuse to acknowledge Me. As I was with the prophet Jeremiah, I am the One who stands beside you. I am the Mighty Warrior who saves. I can take care of all your enemies. In fact, I already did. Why are you still fighting battles that I've already won? The struggles that challenge you are the schemes of your enemy who wants you to think he is in control. Temptations and challenges will arise. But you are safe under My authority. While you may feel alone, I am always standing beside you. Your weapons are not of this world. My strength is with you as you use My name and authority. No one can surpass My power. Your part? Remain faithful to the calling I gave you, resist your enemy, and wear your spiritual armor daily. I am a powerful Warrior, and I was with every great leader and prophet in Scripture. I will lead you to victory too. I will sing over you and quiet you with My love.

FROM A GRATEFUL HEART
Lord, at times I feel so powerless over my enemy's tactics as he tries to capture my thoughts or influence my actions. Sometimes he uses others to tempt me or to taunt my faith words as if they mean nothing. I look around and see no one. I start to panic and feel so alone. And then I remember who You are, and what the message of salvation means to me. By faith, I put on my spiritual armor and cry out to You, the One who is the Mighty Warrior. You envelop me with Your overwhelming presence. I sense Your

breath and Your power, silently assuring me that You are standing here beside me—always. Thank You for rescuing me, time and time again. Thank You for winning the ultimate battle against sin so I could escape spiritual death and inherit eternal life. The enemy behind all desperate schemes and attacks has no hold on me, even though he still tries to deceive. You are my stronghold. Spiritual warfare continues all around me and threatens me daily. But with You beside me, I will not fail. I trust You to bring me through every skirmish my enemy still tries to start. Thank You for fighting my battles with me and for me.

DAILY TRUTH
God never intended for us to fight our battles alone.

DAILY REFLECTIONS
Through you we push back our enemies; through your name we trample our foes. Psalm 44:5 NIV

The weapons we fight with are not the weapons of the world. On the contrary, they have divine power to demolish strongholds. 2 Corinthians 10:4 NIV

But the Lord stands beside me like a great warrior. Before him my persecutors will stumble. They cannot defeat me. They will fail and be thoroughly humiliated. Their dishonor will never be forgotten. Jeremiah 20:11 NLT

"For the Lord your God is the one who goes with you to fight for you against your enemies to give you victory." Deuteronomy 20:4 NIV

DAILY CHALLENGE

Read the song of Moses and the Israelites in Exodus 15:1-19. How was God a warrior for them? What are your most common struggles? What truths in God's Word help you tear down any strongholds and escape any temptations your enemy tries to throw at you? What battles are you fighting that God has already won? Read Ephesians 6:10-18. Every morning as you get dressed, remember to put on your spiritual armor as well. Meditate on 1 John 4:4 and consider memorizing it to help you in your daily struggles.

DAILY THOUGHTS & PRAYERS

Day 74

When You're Stuck in the Now
The One Who Is Eternal

*"The eternal God is your refuge,
and his everlasting arms are under you."*
Deuteronomy 33:27 NLT

FROM YOUR FAITHFUL FATHER'S HEART
My child, you have no concept of what *eternal* means. As hard as your finite mind tries, you can't move beyond the bounds of your own existence yet. You can only see with your earthly eyes. But I have placed eternity in your heart—a hunger that longs to know and experience that which you can only imagine. And one day when you pass from death to eternal life, you will know, and you will understand that I am the meaning of eternal. I am the Beginning and the End. Time means nothing to Me except a momentary blip on the screen of eternity. I am the One who is eternal and I am forever your Refuge during your journey here on this earth. I will show you how to live each day with an eternal emphasis. What you do here with a heart that is on mission for Me will last. Everything else will pass away.

FROM A GRATEFUL HEART
Lord, I rush from one day to another, one project to another, and one moment to another as if I am trying to convince You of my usefulness. Days pass too quickly, and meaningful relationships suffer, simply because I am stuck in the now. Yet, as I think about You and Your eternal nature, I realize that You are far too "other-worldly" for me to understand. I want to know You. I want to experience even a fraction of eternity in my heart, but legs of flesh and a distracted heart often pull me away from You in temporary pursuits. Lord, draw me back into the safety of Your arms. It's You I long for. You are the place where eternity begins. And as my Eternal God and Refuge, You are giving me a heavenly taste of forever if I will simply rest in You. Build Your character in me, and help me to make every thought, every

action, and every word count for You. Help me to grow in my intimacy with You. Show me the activities You have designed for me, those pursuits which will bring You glory and make a difference for all eternity.

DAILY TRUTH
The Holy Spirit is God's gift of eternity in our hearts right now.

DAILY REFLECTIONS
There's far more here than meets the eye. The things we see now are here today, gone tomorrow. But the things we can't see now will last forever. 2 Corinthians 4:18 MSG

Teach us to number our days and recognize how few they are; help us to spend them as we should. Psalm 90:12 TLB

But continue to grow and increase in God's grace and intimacy with our Lord and Savior, Jesus Christ. May he receive all the glory both now and until the day eternity begins. Amen! 2 Peter 3:18 TPT

"I am the Alpha and the Omega—the beginning and the end," says the Lord God. "I am the one who is, who always was, and who is still to come—the Almighty One." Revelation 1:8 NLT

DAILY CHALLENGE
Do you ever feel "stuck in the now"? What kinds of situations or conditions make you feel that way? How does Psalm 90:12 encourage you to make every day count? How has God placed eternity in your heart? (Ecclesiastes 3:11). What are you willing to do to increase your intimacy with God?

DAILY THOUGHTS & PRAYERS

Day 75

When You Think You've Lost Your Way
The One Who Is the Only Way

*Jesus told him, "I am the way, the truth, and the life.
No one can come to the Father except through me."*
John 14:6 NLT

FROM YOUR FAITHFUL FATHER'S HEART

My child, do you think you've lost your way in your grace-filled journey of life? Why do you still struggle with My acceptance of you? Have you been listening to others' voices? Why do you work as if you are still trying to earn My favor? Don't you know there is only one God and one way to enjoy a heavenly relationship? I am the only Way, and I receive you and accept you because of My grace and your faith—not because of who you are or what you do or don't do. My way is a grace gift to be treasured and shared, not a trophy to be earned and displayed. No one is good enough for Me to call "My child." The only way that will happen is by accepting My gift of salvation. Since you've already done that, keep living by faith. Your works will show through naturally when you are connected to Me by faith. It is the only way to true joy and happiness.

FROM A GRATEFUL HEART

Lord, sometimes I regress into spiritual amnesia. Busyness replaces rest, and constant striving tries to steal away the truths on which I began my journey with You. Thoughts of *I'm not good enough* filter through my mind much too often. Thank You for reminding me that I belong to You because of our faith relationship and Your gift of grace, not because of how I feel about myself. And though I want nothing more than to please You through my everyday work and activity, I don't have to depend on any kind of success to make me acceptable in Your sight. I am forever Yours. When that truth seems too good to be true, my heart cries out temporarily, "No Way!" But Your quick response is "Yes, Way!" You are still the One who is the only

Way: the only way to peace, joy, purpose, and a deep, spiritual friendship with my heavenly Creator!

DAILY TRUTH
God's way is way beyond my human understanding.

DAILY REFLECTIONS
There is only one God, and he makes people right with himself only by faith. Romans 3:30 NLT

But now God has shown us a different way to heaven—not by "being good enough" and trying to keep his laws, but by a new way (though not new, really, for the Scriptures told about it long ago). Now God says he will accept and acquit us—declare us "not guilty"—if we trust Jesus Christ to take away our sins. And we all can be saved in this same way, by coming to Christ, no matter who we are or what we have been like. Romans 3:21-22 TLB

For you are all children of God through faith in Christ Jesus. Galatians 3:26 NLT

For it is by grace you have been saved, through faith. Ephesians 2:8 NIV

DAILY CHALLENGE
After reviewing the Bible verses for today, how would you characterize a way lived by grace and one without it? Ask God to reveal any ways you may be trying to live by works and not faith—even though you may be unaware of them. What kind of works would you like to flow naturally from your faith in Christ?

DAILY THOUGHTS & PRAYERS

Day 76

When You're Tempted to Be Judge and Jury
The One Who Will One Day Judge the World

*"For he has set a day when he will judge the world
with justice by the man he has appointed.
He has given proof of this to everyone
by raising him from the dead."*
Acts 17:31 NIV

FROM YOUR FAITHFUL FATHER'S HEART
My child, unless you are an official, elected judge who decides cases by the laws of your land, your job assignment doesn't include condemning the actions of others. And even earthly judges have limited power and make mistakes. I did not appoint you to criticize and pass judgment on every person. Because of My holiness and perfect love for everyone, I cannot overlook sin or allow evil to override good. One day I will uncover all impure motives and ungodliness and will judge the hearts of all people. I will vindicate all those who have suffered in My name and those who have trusted in My Son as their Savior. Jesus' death and resurrection paved the way for all to know Me personally. But those who still reject Him will reap the consequences. As the One who will one day judge the world, I will finally right the system of injustice that has plagued the world since the beginning of time.

FROM A GRATEFUL HEART
Lord, the blood of our forefathers has cried out for justice for centuries. Some of us have experienced the victimization, the hatred, and the violence from stony hearts that have remained unchanged. Jesus, Your own precious Son, endured the worst suffering of all. Because of His perfection, He is the One You appointed to be our advocate for justice. You are the One who judges the world, the One who will separate good from evil. You are the One who will call Your children home one day and bring justice and

reward to all those who love Your name and anticipate Your appearing. I confess my impatience and cold heart toward those who hate You. Instead of criticizing others, Lord, fill me with an urgency and caring love to help others turn to You. I pray that all might know You, long for You, and escape Your judgment.

DAILY TRUTH
If we learn to judge ourselves, we won't be judging others.

DAILY REFLECTIONS
"Appoint judges and administrative officials for all the cities the Lord your God is giving you. They will administer justice in every part of the land." Deuteronomy 16:18 TLB

"God blesses those who are persecuted for doing right, for the Kingdom of Heaven is theirs. God blesses you when people mock you and persecute you and lie about you and say all sorts of evil things against you because you are my followers. Be happy about it! Be very glad! For a great reward awaits you in heaven. And remember, the ancient prophets were persecuted in the same way." Matthew 5:10-12 NLT

Righteousness is revealed every time you judge. Because of the strength of your forgiveness, your anger does not break out every day, even though you are a righteous judge. Psalm 7:11 TPT

Now there is in store for me the crown of righteousness, which the Lord, the righteous Judge, will award to me on that day—and not only to me, but also to all who have longed for his appearing. 2 Timothy 4:8 NIV

DAILY CHALLENGE
Today, offer a special prayer for elected officials and rulers across our world. Pray for fairness, wisdom, and the mind of God for each leader. Every time you are tempted to judge or criticize others, pray for them instead.

DAILY THOUGHTS & PRAYERS

Day 77

When You Need to Renew Your Mind
The One Who Transforms You

*Don't copy the behavior and customs of this world,
but let God transform you into a new person
by changing the way you think.*
Romans 12:2 NLT

FROM YOUR FAITHFUL FATHER'S HEART
My child, if you listen to every voice you hear, you'll experience only confusion. You are in this world, but you are not of this world. Others will hate you because they hated Me. I will protect you from the one who wants to destroy you. As a child of Mine, you are different. Don't copy your culture; reflect My character. I will give you the wisdom, the instruction, and the directions you need to live out your life for Me. You have My Word, the Bible, to help you find answers to life's challenges. Read it. Study it. Memorize and meditate on it daily. Let Me transform your life and your thinking patterns so you will imitate Me, not others. I will renew your mind so you can see life from My perspective, not your own or those of others who don't know Me. My Spirit will keep on changing you and giving you life. I will make you more and more like Me so you can reflect My glory.

FROM A GRATEFUL HEART
Lord, it's so easy to get off track at times and to second guess every decision. So many times I've given in to wrong philosophies and opinions. Instead of simply listening and exercising Your wisdom, I adapted to the culture. My heart longs to hear You clearly and to follow You more dearly, Lord. Some still try to convince me: "This is the way!" or "You need to do this!" And sometimes I'm tempted to follow them. But Lord, if their advice doesn't line up with Yours, the results will prove disastrous. I recommit myself to You with a desire for You to renew my mind. You are the One who transforms me. Change me inside and out. I truly want to be like You.

Thank You for patiently working with me. No one else promises to make us brand new, and then follows through. It's true, Lord. You really do.

DAILY TRUTH
Change is never easy. But when God brings it, it's always good.

DAILY REFLECTIONS
"I have given them your word and the world has hated them, for they are not of the world any more than I am of the world. My prayer is not that you take them out of the world but that you protect them from the evil one. They are not of the world, even as I am not of it." John 17:14-16 NIV

So all of us who have had that veil removed can see and reflect the glory of the Lord. And the Lord—who is the Spirit—makes us more and more like him as we are changed into his glorious image. 2 Corinthians 3:18 NLT

The heart of the wise will easily accept instruction. But those who do all the talking are too busy to listen and learn. They'll just keep stumbling ahead into the mess they created. Proverbs 10:8 TPT

Truth's shining light guides me in my choices and decisions; the revelation of your word makes my pathway clear. Psalm 119:105 TPT

DAILY CHALLENGE
Read Philippians 4:8-9. What kind of thoughts contribute to renewed thinking patterns? What happens when you put God's instructions and those thoughts into action? How will you renew your mind this week and allow God to change your thinking habits?

DAILY THOUGHTS & PRAYERS

Day 78

When You Wonder About Your Destiny
The One Who Gives You His Holy Spirit

*And when you believed in Christ, he identified you as his own
by giving you the Holy Spirit, whom he promised long ago.
The Spirit is God's guarantee that he will give us
the inheritance he promised and that he has purchased us
to be his own people. He did this so we would praise and glorify him.*
Ephesians 1:13-14 NLT

FROM YOUR FAITHFUL FATHER'S HEART
My child, do you still wonder about your destiny or your inheritance as a child of Mine? I purchased you with My own blood, so honor Me with your mind, body, and soul. I am the One who gives you My Holy Spirit as a down payment for the wonderful future waiting for you. It's the first installment of what is yet to come. My Spirit is a seal on your heart, a stamp of love and acceptance that cannot be reversed. You never have to earn My favor or try to live on your own. My Spirit is a forever gift to prove not only that you belong to Me, but that I will always be working through you and perfecting you to glorify Me. It guarantees that all My promises to you will be fulfilled. You are safe and secure in Me. The inheritance waiting for you is literally out of this world. It's a vow I ensured with My life.

FROM A GRATEFUL HEART
Lord, what a blessed assurance You have given me. Thank You for Your gift of the Holy Spirit and for the work You have chosen to do in my life. Forgive me for questioning You or for trying to slash through the weeds of my life with dull tools. My work and my future don't depend on my merit but on my willingness to let Your Spirit work through me. I can't wait to enjoy my inheritance from You when my life has ended. On the other hand, You have already filled my life with unspeakable joy, constant companionship, and priceless blessings. I can't spend my inheritance; I can only enjoy it and

bring You glory by telling others about it, so they will want to know You too. You are my greatest treasure, Lord.

DAILY TRUTH
There is no way to measure the true treasure of your inheritance from God.

DAILY REFLECTIONS
He has put his brand upon us—his mark of ownership—and given us his Holy Spirit in our hearts as guarantee that we belong to him and as the first installment of all that he is going to give us. 2 Corinthians 1:22 TLB

You were God's expensive purchase, paid for with tears of blood, so by all means, then, use your body to bring glory to God! 1 Corinthians 6:20 TPT

What we have received is not the spirit of the world, but the Spirit who is from God, so that we may understand what God has freely given us. 1 Corinthians 2:12 NIV

God has raised from death our Lord Jesus, who is the Great Shepherd of the sheep as the result of his blood, by which the eternal covenant is sealed. May the God of peace provide you with every good thing you need in order to do his will, and may he, through Jesus Christ, do in us what pleases him. And to Christ be the glory forever and ever! Hebrews 13:20-21 GNT

DAILY CHALLENGE
Describe the kind of inheritance you would like (or would have liked) to receive from your parents. If you have children, what kind do you want to leave them? Is there anything you can leave them that will last forever? What's the difference between a legacy and an inheritance?

DAILY THOUGHTS & PRAYERS

Day 79

When You Need God's Healing Hand
The One Who Heals You

"I am the Lord. I am the Lord who heals you."
Exodus 15:26 ICB

FROM YOUR FAITHFUL FATHER'S HEART
My child, where do you go when you're hurting? When your heart races, your temperature spikes, or your anger rises, will you cry out to Me? I am the One who heals you. Sometimes I'll use gifted doctors like My servant Luke. Other times I'll stir your faith and miraculously unlock the key to your healing. On other occasions, I'll ask you to wait so I can use your situation for My glory. My grace is sufficient for you. Will you surrender your life in total faith obedience to Me? I will complete what I started in you. I am the One who heals you and makes you whole—body, mind, and spirit, and the One who also miraculously forgives. One day pain and sickness will end. Do you trust Me enough to ask and leave the answer up to Me?

FROM A GRATEFUL HEART
Lord, You are Jehovah Rapha, the One who heals me, and You have the final word on my destiny. Nothing is impossible with You. With one touch or one word, You can make me whole. Even when my faith is weak, my love for You is strong. If I can bring You more glory through healing, then that's what I desire. If You use doctors to make me well, give them wisdom. Ultimately, the healing You give is always miraculous, and You deserve all the praise. I want to spend my years loving You, loving others, and becoming more like You. I believe You still heal today. But even if Your answer is no, or not now, I want Your will to be my will. I not only need and want Your physical healing, Lord, but a thorough, deep-down cleansing—a whole-hearted renewal of all that I am, body, mind, and spirit. Because all that I am is Yours. Use this trial to change my "what-if" faith to a "no-matter-what" faith. And no matter what, I choose to honor You and give You glory.[1]

DAILY TRUTH
Waiting on God is always a learning experience.

DAILY REFLECTIONS
And he said unto me, My grace is sufficient for thee: for my strength is made perfect in weakness. Most gladly therefore will I rather glory in my infirmities, that the power of Christ may rest upon me. 2 Corinthians 12:9 KJV

When he heard this, Jesus said, "This sickness will not end in death. No, it is for God's glory so that God's Son may be glorified through it." John 11:4 NIV

We, too, wait anxiously for that day when God will give us our full rights as his children, including the new bodies he has promised us—bodies that will never be sick again and will never die. Romans 8:23 TLB

Let all that I am praise the Lord; may I never forget the good things he does for me. He forgives all my sins and heals all my diseases. Psalm 103:2-3 NLT

DAILY CHALLENGE
Spend a few moments meditating on Psalm 103. List as many "benefits" or good things you find that the Lord miraculously does for us. Is your faith a "what-if" faith or a "no-matter-what" surrender? What do you want it to be?

DAILY THOUGHTS & PRAYERS

Day 80

When You Need Someone to Talk To
The One Who Invites You to Himself

My heart has heard you say, "Come and talk with me."
And my heart responds, "Lord, I am coming."
Psalm 27:8 NLT

FROM YOUR FAITHFUL FATHER'S HEART
My child, I love to hear you say, "Yes, Lord," when I call. Throughout the day or in the still of the night, when you listen for My impressions and whispers, you will not be disappointed. I am still the One who invites you to Myself. I am always ready to talk. And I am eager to hear your voice and your prayers to Me. As your faithful heavenly Father, I enjoy sweet fellowship with you and all My children. But there are lessons you will miss and words you will not hear unless you quiet your heart and let go of your own schedule. When you open the pages of My Word, you will find My voice speaking softly. My Holy Spirit will personalize those words to your heart and confirm what you need to hear each day. My children recognize My voice, and I will never contradict what is in My Word. When I call, will you be ready to listen? I'm always listening for you.

FROM A GRATEFUL HEART
Precious Father, the first thing I want to hear when I wake up in the morning is the sweetness of Your Spirit's voice. And the last thing I love to hear as my eyes close for the night is the whisper of Your love in the depths of my heart. You don't raise a thundering voice or send a hurricane to force me to listen, though You may use nature to get my attention and speak to my spirit. Forgive me when busyness or neglect crowds out the sound of heaven in my soul. The memories of our time together and the promise of Your welcome invitation are all I need to bring me into Your presence again. Thank You that You are the One who invites me to Yourself. Even when loneliness surrounds me and it seems there is no one to talk to, You

are always there, waiting for sweet communion with me. Your Word is like a hidden treasure to me. I want to go digging into the depths of the Scriptures Your Spirit has inspired. You hear my whispers, my pleas, and my cries. Today, I will command my spirit to be quiet so I can listen for Your voice through Your Word. Speak, Lord. I do want to hear.

DAILY TRUTH
If I cannot hear God, it may be because I am not listening.

DAILY REFLECTIONS
*And he said, "Go out and stand on the mount before the L*ORD*." And behold, the L*ORD *passed by, and a great and strong wind tore the mountains and broke in pieces the rocks before the L*ORD*, but the L*ORD *was not in the wind. And after the wind an earthquake, but the L*ORD *was not in the earthquake. And after the earthquake a fire, but the L*ORD *was not in the fire. And after the fire the sound of a low whisper. And when Elijah heard it, he wrapped his face in his cloak and went out and stood at the entrance of the cave. And behold, there came a voice to him and said, "What are you doing here, Elijah?" 1 Kings 19:11-13 ESV*

*Then the L*ORD *came and stood, and called as at the other times: "Samuel! Samuel!" And Samuel said, "Speak, for Your servant is listening." 1 Samuel 3:10 NASB*

For his Holy Spirit speaks to us deep in our hearts and tells us that we really are God's children. Romans 8:16 TLB

I rejoice in your word like one who discovers a great treasure. Psalm 119:162 NLT

DAILY CHALLENGE
Meditate on Psalm 46:10. What keeps you from carving out time and being still before the Lord? What can you do to help preserve quiet moments with Him so you can hear Him speaking to you through His Word?

DAILY THOUGHTS & PRAYERS

Day 81

When You Need to Know God Cares
The One Who Is Generous to All Who Ask

Scripture reassures us, "No one who trusts God like this—heart and soul—will ever regret it." It's exactly the same no matter what a person's religious background may be: the same God for all of us, acting the same incredibly generous way to everyone who calls out for help.
"Everyone who calls, 'Help, God!' gets help."
Romans 10:11-13 MSG

FROM YOUR FAITHFUL FATHER'S HEART
My child, do you sometimes feel that I don't care about you? Look at the creatures I made. If I provide for them, will I not also care for you? When I speak, all of My creation pause to hear My voice. They know Me well. I am never stingy with My blessings, and I love to bless My children. I am still the One who is generous to all who ask. I love to hear you call on Me. My salvation is for everyone, whoever they are and wherever their place is in life. I will always hear the prayer offered in humility. I am eager to provide your request. Do you need peace? Ask Me in the name of Jesus and according to My will. Do you need rest? I will give that to you. Do you need wisdom? I invite you to experience My faithfulness in providing for you. Many of My children don't have, because they don't ask. But when your requests are unselfish and will bring glory to Me, you can have confidence that I will not only hear, but I will answer in the way that is best for you.

FROM A GRATEFUL HEART
Lord, my impatience often wins, and I assume You are too busy to care. I confess my failure in not coming to You at times when I truly need Your help. I know I can't meet my own needs. Sometimes I simply forget that You are interested in every detail of my life. You've always been there for me. You never shook Your head or turned away when I needed You the most. Help me to pass on the good news that Your generosity and Your

salvation are indeed for everyone. You won't close the door to anyone who wants to become Your child. You hear all of our cries. You provide all of our needs. And what blessings You have in store once You sign our spiritual birth certificate. You are the One who is generous to all who ask, Lord. I'm so glad that includes me.

DAILY TRUTH
Showing generosity to His children is one of God's favorite activities.

DAILY REFLECTIONS
"Look at the birds of the air; they do not sow or reap or store away in barns, and yet your heavenly Father feeds them. Are you not much more valuable than they? Can any one of you by worrying add a single hour to your life? And why do you worry about clothes? See how the flowers of the field grow. They do not labor or spin. Yet I tell you that not even Solomon in all his splendor was dressed like one of these." Matthew 6:26-29 NIV

You do not have because you do not ask God. When you ask, you do not receive, because you ask with wrong motives, that you may spend what you get on your pleasures. James 4:2-3 NIV

So humble yourselves under the mighty power of God, and at the right time he will lift you up in honor. Give all your worries and cares to God, for he cares about you. 1 Peter 5:6-7 NLT

"For I will do whatever you ask me to do when you ask me in my name. And that is how the Son will show what the Father is really like and bring glory to him." John 14:13 TPT

DAILY CHALLENGE

Are there any details of your life you keep to yourself instead of asking God for help and wisdom? Why? How has God been generous to you? What needs do you think God wants to provide for you? Read Psalm 104:1-34 to see how the psalmist described the relationship between God and His creation—including you—and how He cares for them.

DAILY THOUGHTS & PRAYERS

Day 82

When Your Gratitude Is Lacking
The One Who Deserves Your Thanks

Thank GOD! He deserves your thanks.
His love never quits.
Psalm 136:1 MSG

FROM YOUR FAITHFUL FATHER'S HEART
My child, have you forgotten who you are and where you came from? Look around you. What do you see? Your heart will determine that. Do you see My beautiful creation? Or do you focus on the ugliness in the world? Everything you have, all that you own, and everything you are, you owe to Me. I have given you gifts to use for My glory. I sent My Son to die for you to give you power and freedom over sin in your life. You belong to Me, now and forever. I will love you always. And I have promised to meet all your needs. But don't you know that one of your greatest needs is to know and experience My heart and My faithfulness? Don't I deserve your thanks and praise? A genuine thankful attitude will always usher you into My presence. I love to hear your praises, whether in song, silent whispers, or joyful shouts. When your attitude shines with gratitude, you not only bless Me but others too. I wait daily to fellowship with you. Will you meet with Me each day with a heart full of thanksgiving and praise?

FROM A GRATEFUL HEART
Lord, too often I choose complaints instead of contentment. What right do I have to grumble about anything? You have given me everything I will ever need in life: food, shelter, security, salvation, purpose, destiny, and so much more. Yet when things don't go my way, or when difficulties challenge me, I often forget to look up. My grievances stack up like burnt pancakes. I confess my ungratefulness and forgetfulness, Lord. I am so unworthy of Your goodness. Yet You have poured grace into my life until it overflows. How can I even begin to thank You for all You have done for me? Your

faithfulness leaves me breathless, and Your continual blessings throughout my life deserve unwavering gratitude. You offer me a new day filled with fresh compassion and joy daily. Thank You for being such a great God and Father who loves me with all my faults. With my whole heart, I offer You thanks and praise. And may the first words on my lips every morning be, "Thank You, Lord, for another day to love and praise You."

DAILY TRUTH
Contentment doesn't come from right circumstances; it comes from right thinking.

DAILY REFLECTIONS
Your hearts can soar with joyful gratitude when you think of how God made you worthy to receive the glorious inheritance freely given to us by living in the light. Colossians 1:12 TPT

Let your roots grow down into him and draw up nourishment from him. See that you go on growing in the Lord, and become strong and vigorous in the truth you were taught. Let your lives overflow with joy and thanksgiving for all he has done. Colossians 2:7 TLB

You can pass through his open gates with the password of praise. Come right into his presence with thanksgiving. Come bring your thank offering to him and affectionately bless his beautiful name! Psalm 100:4 TPT

Oh, how grateful and thankful I am to the Lord because he is so good. I will sing praise to the name of the Lord who is above all lords. Psalm 7:17 TLB

DAILY CHALLENGE

What causes your thoughts to spiral downward from contentment to complaint? Read Philippians 4:11-12. In what situations did Paul learn contentment? How does a sense of contentment lead to thanksgiving? Start a gratitude journal. List something each day for which you can thank God. Begin every prayer with thanks and praise for God's goodness to you.

DAILY THOUGHTS & PRAYERS

Day 83

When You Long to Know God As Your Father
The One Who Adopts You As His Child

*So you have not received a spirit that makes you fearful slaves.
Instead, you received God's Spirit
when he adopted you as his own children.
Now we call him, "Abba, Father."*
Romans 8:15 NLT

FROM YOUR FAITHFUL FATHER'S HEART
My child, I love to hear you call Me "Father." My adoption plans for you began long before you were born. I created you in My image. Sin ravaged My world, but I placed a longing in your heart for your real home with Me. I chose you to belong to Me, yet the final decision was yours. You could accept or reject Me as your Father. I am the One who adopted you and made you an heir, and I am so glad you chose My plan for your life. Your adoption as My child doesn't compare to your idea of adoption, legalized by an earthly judge. I did not take you from another home. My plan for you is filled with joy, purpose, and hope, not one that depends on keeping rules. And it's all yours. The adoption papers were sealed with the blood of Jesus when He died for you. Why did I choose to adopt you? Because that gave Me great pleasure. You can be assured that what I want for you is always good. I take Fatherhood seriously.

FROM YOUR FAITHFUL FATHER'S HEART
"Abba," "Father." What a beautiful name to call the Creator of the universe! How is that possible, Lord? Why would You even want more children? Isn't Your family large enough? No, Your desire is for all to know You, to love You, and to fellowship with You. And I do long to know You more, Lord. You're my Disciplinarian, but You're always loving. You're my Judge, but You're always fair. You're my Provider, always meeting my needs. You're my Parent, always teaching me truth. You're my heavenly "Daddy," always for-

giving my weaknesses. Of all the names I could call You, Lord, I am most proud to call You Father. Thank You that Jesus paved the way so I could know You as my true Abba, Father. Thank You that You are the One who adopts me as Your child.

DAILY TRUTH
Wherever the faithful Father goes, a grateful child is always following.

DAILY REFLECTIONS
For it was always in his perfect plan to adopt us as his delightful children, through our union with Jesus, the Anointed One, so that his tremendous love that cascades over us would glorify his grace—for the same love he has for the Beloved, Jesus, he has for us. And this unfolding plan brings him great pleasure! Ephesians 1:5 TPT

"For I know the plans I have for you," declares the Lord, "plans to prosper you and not to harm you, plans to give you hope and a future." Jeremiah 29:11 NIV

But when the right time came, God sent his Son, born of a woman, subject to the law. God sent him to buy freedom for us who were slaves to the law, so that he could adopt us as his very own children. And because we are his children, God has sent the Spirit of his Son into our hearts, prompting us to call out, "Abba, Father." Now you are no longer a slave but God's own child. And since you are his child, God has made you his heir. Galatians 4:4-7 NLT

So God created mankind in his own image, in the image of God he created them; male and female he created them. Genesis 1:27 NIV

DAILY CHALLENGE

You may or may not have been adopted by your earthly parents. If you were, you may understand the feeling of being accepted and chosen. But even the best earthly parent can't give us what God promises. List all the ways God is different from any earthly parent.

DAILY THOUGHTS & PRAYERS

Day 84

When You Can't Feel God's Presence
The One Who Is Everywhere

*"Can anyone hide from me in a secret place?
Am I not everywhere in all the heavens and earth?" says the* Lord.
Jeremiah 23:24 NLT

FROM YOUR FAITHFUL FATHER'S HEART
My child, when you can't feel My presence, don't panic. I am the One who is everywhere. Your emotions don't negate who I am or whose you are. Neither do they eradicate My presence in your life. No matter where you search, you can find Me. In the darkest valley, I will shine My light on you. From the highest mountain, you can see My handiwork for miles. Wherever you go, you can find the footprint of My creativity. I am everywhere. You can never escape My presence. My omnipresence hovers near you wherever you are. Your enemy may try to erect a wall between us to discourage you, but he can never snatch you away from Me. Call on Me, and I will hear you. Unconfessed sin in your life may quench My Spirit, break our fellowship, and create distance between us. But I will be faithful to show you the way back. I have promised to never leave or forsake you. Remember that I am still the faithful One who never changes. Let your prayers and your praise rise to Me with confidence, because I am the One who lives in your heart, night and day.

FROM A GRATEFUL HEART
Lord, still the lies when I sometimes question Your presence. My enemy loves to point his finger at me and accuse me of hypocrisy. Sometimes he tries to weave false guilt into the fabric of my life when I can't seem to find You. Help me turn my heart to You and Your Word as I listen once again to the truths You want me to hear. You are always with me, and in me, because I belong to You. Thank You for Your faithful promises, for pursuing me passionately, and for loving me even when my emotions go awry. Your

patience and longsuffering always accompany Your faithfulness. What a comfort and joy to know that You are the One who is everywhere. At times my selfishness begs for dark corners or distant places to escape Your penetrating gaze. But You are the God who loves me even in my weak moments and draws me back to Yourself. I delight in Your presence, Your protection, and Your precious plan for my life. Knowing that wherever I go, not only have You already been there, but You are still there, encouraging me, guiding me, and watching over me, frees me to live in joyful abandonment to You.

DAILY TRUTH
We can never escape God's presence.

DAILY REFLECTIONS
For hasn't he promised you, "I will never leave you alone, never! And I will not loosen my grip on your life!" Hebrews 13:5 TPT

I can never escape from your Spirit! I can never get away from your presence! If I go up to heaven, you are there; if I go down to the grave, you are there. If I ride the wings of the morning, if I dwell by the farthest oceans, even there your hand will guide me, and your strength will support me. Psalm 139:7-10 NLT

"You will search for me. And when you search for me with all your heart, you will find me!" Jeremiah 29:13 ICB

If we confess our sins, he is faithful and just to forgive us our sins, and to cleanse us from all unrighteousness. 1 John 1:9 KJV

DAILY CHALLENGE

Do you know Jesus as your personal Savior and Lord? If so, when you doubt His presence, are you basing your feelings on your emotions, rather than on God's faithfulness and the penalty Jesus already paid for you? If your answer to the first question is no, pause and ask Jesus to forgive you and to come into your heart. (Check out the help in the back of this book, *Begin The Journey*). If you do know Jesus, ask Him to show you any unconfessed sin so you can draw closer to Him. For a child of God, continual confession brings restoration of fellowship and growth in Him. Thank God for His constant presence, whether you feel His nearness or not.

DAILY THOUGHTS & PRAYERS

Day 85

When You Need Unfailing Love
The One Whose Unfailing Love Never Ends

*Your unfailing love will last forever.
Your faithfulness is as enduring as the heavens.*
Psalm 89:2 NLT

FROM YOUR FAITHFUL FATHER'S HEART

My child, unfailing love and faithfulness are part of My character. At times you will question My loyalty. Will I fail you? Will I leave you to work out your life on your own? Am I dependable? But never base your perspective on circumstances or feelings. In this world, you will experience heartbreak, trials, and yes, even discipline that seems harsh to you. During those times you may be thinking those are the realities of life. And you can't see an end to them. Keep remembering that I am the One whose unfailing love never ends. Faithful is who I am. And faithfulness is what I do. Everything serves its purpose in My eyes. The world as you know it today is like a theater with changing scenes and characters. It will soon pass away and all the hurt and pain with it. But My unfailing love is like an eternal sunrise that never goes down. My love for you is without borders. It knows no limits. I am the One whose unfailing love never ends. My love is forever.

FROM A GRATEFUL HEART

Lord, sometimes I've allowed painful circumstances to cloud my view of who You really are. How could I ever doubt Your love for me? In a thousand ways You assure me of Your faithful love daily. And when I stop and listen to You instead of giving in to my circumstances, the truth always shines through. Your unfailing love is sewn into the very fabric of my life. Your faithfulness reaches to the heavens. I can't touch it. I can't see it. Sometimes I can't even feel it, because my earthly frustrations have numbed my spiritual perspective. But Lord, by faith I believe You are the One whose unfailing love never ends. And in that knowledge and belief, I have confidence,

You always have my back. Jesus' death on the cross settled that unfailing love issue long ago.

DAILY TRUTH
To God, love is not a feeling. It is His unchanging character.

DAILY REFLECTIONS
Your unfailing love, O Lord, is as vast as the heavens; your faithfulness reaches beyond the clouds. Psalm 36:5 NLT

The Lord works everything together to accomplish his purpose. Proverbs 16:4 TPT

For this world as we know it will soon pass away. 1 Corinthians 7:31 NLT

For I am convinced [and continue to be convinced—beyond any doubt] that neither death, nor life, nor angels, nor principalities, nor things present and threatening, nor things to come, nor powers, nor height, nor depth, nor any other created thing, will be able to separate us from the [unlimited] love of God, which is in Christ Jesus our Lord. Romans 8:38-39 AMP

DAILY CHALLENGE
When are you most tempted to question God's love? What does His Word say about His love for you? Today, start your own list: *Ways God Shows Me His Unfailing Love.* Use the Bible verses in today's devotions to help you begin. Then each time you find a reason in God's Word, or experience a practical way He shows you His love, jot it down and review that list often.

DAILY THOUGHTS & PRAYERS

Day 86

When You're Feeling Needy
The One Who Satisfies Every Need

"He himself gives life and breath to everything, and he satisfies every need."
Acts 17:25 NLT

FROM YOUR FAITHFUL FATHER'S HEART
My child, I'm always here for you. Don't hesitate to tell Me your needs. If you had no needs or problems, how would you know whether I could supply them? How would you experience My faithfulness if you didn't allow Me the pleasure of nurturing our intimate Father/child relationship? Food, shelter, clothing? Love, security, acceptance, forgiveness? Your daily bread? No matter what you ask, if it's something good for you, I am the One who satisfies every need in your life. Because I know you so well, I know exactly what you need, and I want you to trust Me completely for that provision. Instead of working feverishly as if it all depended on you, rest in your faithful Father's promises. When you surrender your life to Me, I will bless the work of your hands and the intent of your heart. If I provide for all My creation, why would I not satisfy your needs, too?

FROM A GRATEFUL HEART
Lord, lately it seems like all I do is run to You in my neediness. "Lord, would You do this? Would You provide this? God, could You make this happen? Would You help my friend?" And just like a loving Father should, You listen. You hear my cries. And You hold me even when it's hard for me to see a way through the mountain of needs. As I look back through the years, I recognize Your faithful footprints on my heart and Your amazing work in my life. You've always been available when I call, and You've never left me alone to solve my problems on my own. You are truly the One who satisfies every need, in Your time, and in Your way. Whether it's a spiritual, physical, or emotional need, You are the faithful One I turn to, Lord, again

and again. You are the only One who knows me so well and what is truly best for me. Thank You for Your daily manna, and most of all, for Your eternal salvation.

DAILY TRUTH
God is your Jehovah Jireh—your faithful provider.

DAILY REFLECTIONS
Give us this day our daily bread. Matthew 6:11 KJV

"He fed you with manna in the wilderness (it was a kind of bread unknown before) so that you would become humble and so that your trust in him would grow, and he could do you good." Deuteronomy 8:16 TLB

And Abraham called the name of that place Jehovahjireh: as it is said to this day, In the mount of the Lord it shall be seen. Genesis 22:14 KJV

I am convinced that my God will fully satisfy every need you have, for I have seen the abundant riches of glory revealed to me through Jesus Christ! Philippians 4:19 TPT

DAILY CHALLENGE
How has God provided for you? In what ways did He supply those needs? Take time to express your thanks to God for His constant provision. List your greatest, current needs. If it helps, divide them up into categories like spiritual, emotional, and physical. One by one, talk to God about them. Let Him know you are trusting Him to supply those needs.

DAILY THOUGHTS & PRAYERS

Day 87

When You Want to Be More Than a Number
The One Who Knows Your Name

"I have called you by name; you are mine."
Isaiah 43:1 NLT

FROM YOUR FAITHFUL FATHER'S HEART
My child, you are more than a number to Me. I can count the number of stars in the universe, and I call them by name. After all, I created them and flung them onto the velvet black canopy of space. But you hold a more valuable place in My heart than those beautiful, twinkling lights. I am the One who knows your name too. I know the number of hairs on your head. But our relationship is not an arithmetic challenge. I love you as My supreme, crowning creation. I created you a little lower than the angels for My glory and to enjoy fellowship with Me. And I chose you personally, calling out your name, inviting you to become My child. The next time you doubt how I feel about you, look up at the billions of evening stars. You can try to count them, but that's impossible for you. If I know each of their names, do you not think I can remember yours?

FROM A GRATEFUL HEART
Lord, I refuse to live as if I were the last person chosen on a sports team. I am not the least; I am not the best. I am Yours. And I don't need to take a number and stand in line to enter Your presence. You make me feel as if I am enough for You just as I am. I don't need to shout, beg, or cry for a hearing with You. You never jog Your memory about who I am. You are the One who knows my name and everything about me. And that's true about all Your children. When I'm feeling low or discouraged, unimportant or de-valued, I simply remember that I belong to You. You created me; You know everything about me, past, present, and future. I am not just a number lost in creation. You have given me a purpose and value, and I am loved by the One who created me. And because Jesus' death covered my sin, You

accepted me as Your child. How is that possible? You are amazing, God.

DAILY TRUTH
Anonymous is not a word in God's vocabulary.

DAILY REFLECTIONS
He counts the stars and calls them all by name. Psalm 147:4 NLT

God made the two great lights—the greater light (the sun) to rule the day, and the lesser light (the moon) to rule the night; He made the [galaxies of] stars also [that is, all the amazing wonders in the heavens]. God placed them in the expanse of the heavens to provide light upon the earth, to rule over the day and the night, and to separate the light from the darkness; and God saw that it was good and He affirmed and sustained it. Genesis 1:16-18 AMP

I look at the heavens, which you made with your hands. I see the moon and stars, which you created. But why is man important to you? Why do you take care of human beings? You made man a little lower than the angels. And you crowned him with glory and honor. Psalm 8:3-5 ICB

"But the true Shepherd walks right up to the gate, and because the gatekeeper knows who he is, he opens the gate to let him in. And the sheep recognize the voice of the true Shepherd, for he calls his own by name and leads them out, for they belong to him. And when he has brought out all his sheep, he walks ahead of them and they will follow him, for they are familiar with his voice." John 10:2-4 TPT

DAILY CHALLENGE

The psalmist uses our place in creation to express our value to God. Read Luke 12:7. Why is this number a positive one? What other comparison did Jesus use to prove our value? What does He compare us to in John 10:2-4? How do those analogies make you feel? Research some well-known stars and their names. Multiply the number of those by billions of others God created. Thank God that He knows your name just like He knows the names of each star.

DAILY THOUGHTS & PRAYERS

Day 88

When Heaven Seems Near
The One Who Will Take You to Heaven

We tell you this directly from the Lord: We who are still living when the Lord returns will not meet him ahead of those who have died. For the Lord himself will come down from heaven with a commanding shout, with the voice of the archangel, and with the trumpet call of God. First, the believers who have died will rise from their graves. Then, together with them, we who are still alive and remain on the earth will be caught up in the clouds to meet the Lord in the air. Then we will be with the Lord forever.
1 Thessalonians 4:15-17 NLT

FROM YOUR FAITHFUL FATHER'S HEART
My child, as the years pass, heaven grows nearer. When you see pain and confusion in your world, do you question if life is worth the effort? One day the call will come; the trumpet will sound, and I, as your Savior and Lord, will return for My children. Whether you are still living or not, I will take you with Me—you and all the other believers from the four corners of the earth who have died before you. These and all My children still alive will meet Me in the air and live with Me forever. Never give up hope. Stay prepared, and remain faithful until the end of your days. You are not working for rewards, though your service will be rewarded. You can't earn your place in heaven. But you can follow Me and live for Me as long as I give you life. I want you to experience the joy of My presence forever. Hold on, My child. It won't be long. Never fear death or future events. I am the One who will take you to heaven.

FROM A GRATEFUL HEART
Lord, the signs of Your return are growing clearer, and heaven is growing nearer. Some days I want to remain here so I can help others find You and experience Your deep love. I want them to know You've prepared a place

for them if they will only believe. Other times, my body, mind, and spirit are so tired, I long for heaven now. None of us know when our days will end, or when You will return. But what a day that will be, when we finally get to see You and live with You forever. Whether You return today or a thousand years from now, I choose to focus on loving and serving You. You are the One who will take me to heaven. What a hallelujah chorus that will be when I finally see You face to face and accompany You as part of a great choir, soaring our way home!

DAILY TRUTH
Heaven is where our hearts will finally be at home.

DAILY REFLECTIONS
"So always be ready, alert, and prepared, because at an hour when you're not expecting him, the Son of Man will come." Matthew 24:44 TPT

And when Christ who is our real life comes back again, you will shine with him and share in all his glories. Colossians 3:4 TLB

May the God of peace himself make you entirely pure and devoted to God; and may your spirit and soul and body be kept strong and blameless until that day when our Lord Jesus Christ comes back again. 1 Thess 5:23 TLB

"His master replied, 'Well done, good and faithful servant! You have been faithful with a few things; I will put you in charge of many things. Come and share your master's happiness!'" Matthew 25:23 NIV

DAILY CHALLENGE
What kind of emotions arise when you think about death? Review John 14:1-4. Then Read 1 Thessalonians 4:13. How do all these Bible verses today help reduce the fear of dying for you? Or the death of others? Because of Jesus, what can you look forward to? How are you preparing for your home in heaven now? What signs do you see in your world today that could indicate Christ's soon return?

DAILY THOUGHTS & PRAYERS

Day 89

When You Long to Give God Praise
The One Whose Name Is Above All Others

*Let them praise the name of the Lord
because his name is high above all others.
His glory is above heaven and earth.*
Psalm 148:13 GW

FROM YOUR FAITHFUL FATHER'S HEART
My child, if someone were to compile a list of great people on earth, you'd expect to see presidents, musicians, athletes, and others with wide influence. But often one grave error can send those names to the trash heap or gossip column of a magazine. My name never fades. I am still the One whose name is above all others, not because of what I do, though others have celebrated My works and miracles throughout the ages. My name is great because of who I am. But I invite you to experience more of My greatness and faithfulness. Because of My Son's sacrifice for all, the name of Jesus—who is God by nature—is the name above all names. I love to hear your praise, My child. Praise opens your heart to the joy and blessings I have already prepared for you daily.

FROM A GRATEFUL HEART
Lord, when I think of greatness, You are the only One that word defines. You are the One whose name is above all others. Nations rise and fall because of You. Lives are changed and rearranged at the very mention of Your name. Your name scatters demons and worthless idols and invites blessing and honor. Your name, and the name of Jesus, like Your power, are beyond description. Sometimes gratitude and thanksgiving for You swell in my heart so large, I feel like a balloon about to burst. I long to give You praise. My hands raise; my knees fall; my body trembles, and I wish for a thousand tongues to speak Your awesome name in praise, for You are the only One worthy of it. May praise for You ever be on my lips and in my heart.

DAILY TRUTH
Greatness belongs to God alone.

DAILY REFLECTIONS
My heart explodes with praise to you! Now and forever my heart bows in worship to you, my King and my God! Every day I will lift up my praise to your name with praises that will last throughout eternity. Lord, you are great and worthy of the highest praise! For there is no end to the discovery of the greatness that surrounds you. Psalm 145:1-3 TPT

"He alone is your God, the only one who is worthy of your praise, the one who has done these mighty miracles that you have seen with your own eyes." Deuteronomy 10:21 NLT

I will praise you as long as I live, and in your name I will lift up my hands. Psalm 63:4 NIV

Have this attitude in yourselves which was also in Christ Jesus, who, as He already existed in the form of God, did not consider equality with God something to be grasped, but emptied Himself by taking the form of a bond-servant and being born in the likeness of men. And being found in appearance as a man, He humbled Himself by becoming obedient to the point of death: death on a cross. For this reason also God highly exalted Him, and bestowed on Him the name which is above every name, so that at the name of Jesus EVERY KNEE WILL BOW, of those who are in heaven and on earth and under the earth, and that every tongue will confess that Jesus Christ is Lord, to the glory of God the Father. Philippians 2:5-11 NASB

DAILY CHALLENGE

What was Jesus' attitude when He came to earth? Why is this important in how we feel about God and how we praise Him? Listen to a favorite hymn or praise song. Spend a few moments simply thanking and praising God today for who He is.

DAILY THOUGHTS & PRAYERS

Day 90

When You're Longing for More Joy
The One Who Makes Your Joy Overflow

*"I have told you these things so that My joy
and delight may be in you, and that your joy may be made
full and complete and overflowing."*
John 15:11 AMP

FROM YOUR FAITHFUL FATHER'S HEART

My child, happiness is temporary. Earthly treasures like cars, jewelry, or expensive technology may bring you false security, and they will never bring you lasting joy. Great wealth can even cause trouble if you cling to it and let it drive you to want more. Even simple pleasures, like home and family, though they are truly blessings from My hand, can never completely satisfy the deepest longings in your heart. I am the only One who can fill that void. Not only am I the One who makes your joy overflow, but My faithful love and the pleasure of My company last forever. From the time you begin to follow Me, I will unfold your personal road map, little by little, while walking beside you all the way. My fellowship is like no other. Enjoy My faithful presence daily!

FROM A GRATEFUL HEART

Lord, how foolish I've been at times to think that things could satisfy. I succumb to temptations hidden beneath the allurement of online or department store sales or ads for expensive devices. Sometimes I seek ungodly advice instead of searching for what You have promised to give if only I'll ask. And in the end, none of those pursuits bring joy, but only disappointment—and sometimes debt. Forgive me for sidetracks that take me nowhere fast. You truly are the only One who makes my joy overflow, Lord. How I love to relax in Your presence. Thank You for giving me the promise and the pleasure of Your company, both now—and forever.

DAILY TRUTH
Each time we step into God's presence, we get a glimpse of unspeakable joy.

DAILY REFLECTIONS
It's much better to live simply, surrounded in holy awe and worship of God, than to have great wealth with a home full of trouble. Proverbs 15:16 TPT

But let the godly rejoice. Let them be glad in God's presence. Let them be filled with joy. Psalm 68:3 NLT

*The revelation of G*OD *is whole and pulls our lives together. The signposts of G*OD *are clear and point out the right road. The life-maps of G*OD *are right, showing the way to joy. The directions of G*OD *are plain and easy on the eyes. G*OD*'s reputation is twenty-four-carat gold, with a lifetime guarantee. The decisions of G*OD *are accurate down to the nth degree. Psalm 19:7-9 MSG*

Satisfy us in the morning with Your faithful love so that we may shout with joy and be glad all our days. Psalm 90:14 HCSB

DAILY CHALLENGE
Where have you looked for happiness? Has anything tried to steal your joy? What brings you the greatest fulfillment? List some of the things that come to mind. Describe the kind of joy you want to experience. Ask God to show you anything you have allowed into your life that has sidetracked you from the kind of joy He wants to give you. How has God made your joy overflow?

DAILY THOUGHTS & PRAYERS

Begin the Journey

Perhaps you have never come to know and enjoy the intimate presence of God personally. If He has placed such a desire in your heart, may I share with you some simple steps so you can become acquainted with Him and become a child of God forever?

1. Admit the sin in your life and the need in your heart for God (see Romans 3:23).
2. Acknowledge that Jesus loves you and that He died for your sin (see John 3:16).
3. Recognize His salvation is a gift, not something earned (see Ephesians 2:8-9; Romans 6:23).
4. Ask Jesus to forgive you, to come into your life, and to fill you with His personal, intimate presence (see John 1:12).
5. By faith, thank Him that you are now God's child, and confess that from now on, He will be the Lord and Love of your life. Give Jesus the keys to all the rooms of your heart (see Romans 10:9-10; John 1:12).

I'm praying for you as you begin your journey. For more information, see my website: **www.rebeccabarlowjordan.com** *or* **www.day-votions.com**.

Day-votedly His, Rebecca

Bible Versions and Translations

Scripture quotations marked AMP are taken from the Amplified® Bible (AMP), Copyright © 2015 by The Lockman Foundation. Used by permission. www.lockman.org.

Scripture quotations marked CEB are taken from the COMMON ENGLISH BIBLE. © Copyright 2011 COMMON ENGLISH BIBLE. All rights reserved. Used by permission.

Scripture quotations marked CEV are from the Contemporary English Version Copyright © 1991, 1992, 1995 by American Bible Society, Used by Permission.

Scripture quotations marked ESV are from the ESV® Bible (The Holy Bible, English Standard Version®), copyright © 2001 by Crossway, a publishing ministry of Good News Publishers. Used by permission. All rights reserved.

Scripture quotations marked GNT are from the Good News Translation in Today's English Version—Second Edition Copyright © 1992 by American Bible Society. Used by Permission.

Scripture quotations marked GW are taken from *God's Word*® © 1995 by God's Word to the Nations. Used by permission of Baker Publishing Group.

Scripture quotations marked HCSB are taken from the Holman Christian Standard Bible®, Copyright © 1999, 2000, 2002, 2003, 2009 by Holman Bible Publishers. Used by permission. Holman Christian Standard Bible®, Holman CSB®, and HCSB® are federally registered trademarks of Holman Bible Publishers.

Scripture quotations marked ICB are taken from the International Children's Bible®. Copyright © 1986, 1988, 1999 by Thomas Nelson. Used by permission. All rights reserved.

Scripture quotations marked ISV are taken from the Holy Bible: International Standard Version® Release 2.0. Copyright © 1996-2013 by the ISV Foundation. Used by permission of Davidson Press, LLC. ALL RIGHTS RESERVED INTERNATIONALLY.

Scripture quotations marked KJV are from the King James Version of the Bible.

Scripture quotations marked TLB are taken from The Living Bible copyright © 1971. Used by permission of Tyndale House Publishers, Carol Stream, Illinois 60188. All rights reserved.

Scripture quotations marked MSG are taken from THE MESSAGE, copyright © 1993, 2002, 2018 by Eugene H. Peterson. Used by permission of NavPress, represented by Tyndale House Publishers. All rights reserved.

Scripture quotations marked NASB are taken from the NASB® New American Standard Bible®, Copyright © 1960, 1971, 1977, 1995, 2020 by The Lockman Foundation. Used by permission. All rights reserved. www.lockman.org.

Scripture quotations marked NIrV are taken from the Holy Bible, New International Reader's Version®, NIrV® Copyright © 1995, 1996, 1998, 2014 by Biblica, Inc.® Used by permission of Zondervan. All rights reserved worldwide. www.zondervan.com The "NIrV" and "New International Reader's Version" are trademarks registered in the United States Patent and Trademark Office by Biblica, Inc.®

Scripture quotations marked NIV are taken from the Holy Bible, New International Version®, NIV®. Copyright © 1973, 1978, 1984, 2011 by Biblica, Inc.® Used by permission of Zondervan. All rights reserved worldwide. www.zondervan.com The "NIV" and "New International Version" are trademarks registered in the United States Patent and Trademark Office by Biblica, Inc.®

Scripture quotations marked NKJV are taken from the New King James Version®. Copyright © 1982 by Thomas Nelson. Used by permission. All rights reserved.

Scripture quotations marked NLT are taken from the Holy Bible, New Living Translation, copyright ©1996, 2004, 2015 by Tyndale House Foundation. Used by permission of Tyndale House Publishers, Carol Stream, Illinois 60188. All rights reserved.

Scripture quotations marked TPT are from The Passion Translation®. Copyright © 2017, 2018 by Passion & Fire Ministries, Inc. Used by permission. All rights reserved. ThePassionTranslation.com.

Scripture quotations marked VOICE are taken from The Voice™. Copyright © 2012 by Ecclesia Bible Society. Used by permission. All rights reserved.

Acknowledgments

I am so grateful for the faithfulness of family and friends who prayed for me during the crafting and publishing of this book. A special thanks to those who gave their time and counsel to help me decide on several issues in the beginning: Kathy Kirkpatrick, Jennifer Hanson, Karen Walker, Barbara Karbowski, Shawn McEvoy, Julie Robinson, Wendy Wagley, Fran Sandin, Rosemary Gray, and Priscilla Adams.

Thanks to Rob Eagar for his helpful consultation and marketing resources, and Susan Neal and the CIPA (Christian Indie Publishing Association) for additional publishing helps. I also appreciate so many friends who encouraged me throughout this writing process, who answered many of my questions, and who prayed for my writing.

Thank you to those who so graciously endorsed this book, even adding their expertise and suggestions.

Special thanks to my cover and interior designers, Ken Raney, (whose wife, Deborah, is one of my favorite fiction authors), and Collin Smith, both talented artists who designed a beautiful work.

Thank you to my family for their prayers and gracious support. And I could never have finished this project without the love, prayers, encouragement, and editing help from my amazing husband Larry—who inspires me to seek God's heart daily and understands my desire to write about God's faithfulness.

But above all, I offer deep gratitude to my heavenly Father whose unconditional love and unchangeable faithfulness never ends and who has allowed me the joy of His intimate, daily presence.

Notes

Introduction

1. A. W. Tozer, *Tozer on the Almighty God,* compiled by Ron Eggert (Camp Hill, Pennsylvania: Christian Publications, 2004), June 16.

Day 69

1. Adapted from the blog post by Rebecca Barlow Jordan, 2017. "A Prayer for Anxiety and Stress," last modified July 30, 2021, https://www.rebeccabarlowjordan.com/prayer-for-anxiety-and-stress/.

Day 79

1. Adapted from the blog post by Rebecca Barlow Jordan, 2015. "When You Need God's Divine Healing - A Personal Prayer," last modified on April 6, 2017, https://www.rebeccabarlowjordan.com/when-you-need-gods-divine-healing-personal-prayer/.

About Rebecca

Rebecca Barlow Jordan is a day-voted follower of Jesus whose passion is helping others find joy and purposeful living through deeper intimacy with God. A CBA bestselling, inspirational author, Rebecca has authored, co-authored, and contributed to over 30 books, including the popular *Daily in Your Presence* devotional. In addition, she has sold over 2000 greeting cards, devotions, articles, and other inspirational pieces and is a frequent contributor to crosswalk.com.

Rebecca is a minister's wife and has two daughters and four grandchildren. When she's not writing, she enjoys gardening, reading, fishing, spending time with family, and learning about the Father's heart where she lives in Texas.

In 2008, Hardin-Simmons University awarded Rebecca the Distinguished Alumni Award. From years of Bible study and teaching experience, she paints encouragement on the hearts of others through her books and other writings, including her inspirational blog and website, where you can connect with her at **rebeccabarlowjordan.com** or **day-votions.com**.

~

If this book has blessed and encouraged you, I would love to hear from you. Would you also consider writing a review on Amazon, Goodreads, or any other online retailers where this book is sold? Together, we can be a team sharing God's faithfulness and helping to encourage others toward deeper intimacy with God. I would deeply appreciate your help.

Take advantage of my free eBook when you sign up for my weekly newsletter, blog updates, and special news at **www.rebeccabarlowjordan.com**. And while you're there, check out my other inspirational devotional books.

Day-votedly His, *Rebecca*

Made in the USA
Monee, IL
19 January 2023